THE WORLD'S GREATEST
GOLF COURSES

THE WORLD'S GREATEST
GOLF COURSES

A comprehensive guide to golf courses around the world

Geoffrey Giles

First published by Parragon in 2008

Parragon
Queen Street House
4 Queen Street
Bath BA1 1HE, UK

Copyright © Parragon Books Ltd 2008

Created and produced by JOLLANDS EDITIONS
Design JC LANAWAY
Course maps COMPARE INFOBASE LIMITED

ISBN 978-1-4075-3910-2

Printed in China

PRACTICAL DETAILS

Most of the courses in this book welcome visiting golfers, the exceptions being some private clubs, mainly in the United States and Canada. The famous championship courses are inundated with requests to play so book well in advance. Club websites will usually include details of fees, availability, handicap restrictions, dress codes, and whether a letter of introduction is required, and many will have an online booking facility.

Distances in the book are given in yards, which are used in North America and – still, despite metrication – by the golfing community in Great Britain.

Scorecards give the hole lengths from the back or championship tees as they were at the time of writing. Note that, for championships, what might be a short par 5 for the members is sometimes re-designated as a long par 4 for competitors. Clubs frequently build new tees or simply remeasure their course, so these distances should only be used as a guideline.

Every effort has been made to check facts thoroughly, but errors may have crept in. The publisher would be grateful for corrections or information helpful for future editions.

▶▶▶ Contents

▶▶▶ Introduction

It was the great English-born American golf course designer Robert Trent Jones who wrote, 'The first golf course architect, of course, was the Lord, and he was the best there has ever been.' The early golfers of Scotland and the Netherlands played their golf on relatively undefined patches of ground wherever they happened to live. There was no such thing as a typical golf course. And while a few elements of a course have become standardized, there is still no standard golf course.

The Scots became the defining influence on golf when the Honourable Company of Edinburgh Golfers laid down the first set of rules in 1744. In 1754 twenty-two 'Noblemen and Gentlemen' gathered in St Andrews to form the Royal and Ancient Golf Club of St Andrews (R&A), and the newcomers gradually gained the ascendancy. Their rules dealt mainly with the situations that might occur during the course of a match – the rules of matchplay. You played against each other, not against the course. Medal play would have been unthinkable, because the number of holes per course varied until St Andrews, which had now reduced its course to one of 18 holes, standardized this number for a round of golf in 1858.

ABOVE *The spiritual home of golf, St Andrews. The R&A does not own the golf courses – the Old Course is one of several run by the Links Management Trust on behalf of the town. Visitors may book online, by post or by telephone far in advance, take advantage of one of the golf tour operators' packages, or take pot luck in one of the daily ballots.*

BELOW *Royal County Down, originally laid out by Old Tom Morris over 100 years ago.*

In the mid-19th century men began to 'design' golf courses. The great players of the day were called upon to lay out the 'links' of newly formed golf clubs. Those great players were all Scottish and they all played on the links courses of Scotland, on that strip of unfertile, sandy soil between the beach and the town or farmland. Inevitably they tried to recreate the features that gave their home courses distinction. They looked for green sites in hollows, which would be self-watering with dew, or on humps and hillocks, because they tested technique. Sand exposed by sheep sheltering from the wind or natural erosion had become a common feature of links, and these were replicated by early bunkers.

ABOVE *Cape Kidnappers, New Zealand – an example of the work of American designer Tom Doak. Doak has an unerring talent for locating stunning green sites and keeping the golfer thinking until the very last putt has dropped.*

Today's golf course designers are master craftsmen, and they are doing just what Allan Robertson, Tom Morris and Willie Park did a century and a half ago. They now have the benefit of computer-aided design, sophisticated earth-moving machines, real-estate lawyers, civil engineers and environmentalists. Given the restraints of what they may be allowed to do, ecologically, and the dire consequences of getting it the tiniest bit wrong, we should rejoice that the greatest players of our day are prepared to emulate Robertson, Morris and Park.

▶▶▶ Courses 1–20

▶▶▶ Great Britain & Ireland

Scotland is the cradle of golf. The game was enjoyed there in the Middle Ages, and it is recorded that golf was played in England in 1608 by Scots attached to the court of King James I of England (James VI of Scotland) at Blackheath. However, golf in the British Isles must be judged by the courses of the 21st century, of which there are about 3,000.

Some of these are historic: the Old Course at St Andrews, Royal Liverpool, Royal County Down. Some are state of the art: Celtic Manor, the Belfry, the K-Club. But it is the quality of the courses that do not make the 'Top 10 Charts' that illustrates the strength in depth of golf courses in the UK and Ireland.

Nowhere in the world can boast finer – or more profuse – links or heathland courses. Yet there are so many other choice terrains – downland, fenland, moorland, and ancestral parkland. For the most part these have been exploited by the great architects of the Golden Age: Harry Colt, Alister MacKenzie, Herbert Fowler, George Abercromby, Tom Simpson. Contemporary giants have not been slow in following suit.

St Andrews

St Andrews

The Old Course, St Andrews, Fife, Scotland

There is no more famous golfing town than St Andrews. It is, after all, the Home of Golf, and the game has been played there since the 15th century. Overlooking the Old Course is the handsome clubhouse of the Royal and Ancient Golf Club (R&A), a comparative newcomer to St Andrews having been founded in 1754. Nowadays the R&A governs the game throughout the world, with the exception of North America, and every five years it brings its Open Championship (or British Open, as it is widely known through the golfing world) to the Old Course, producing winners of the calibre of Tiger Woods, Jack Nicklaus, Severiano Ballesteros and Nick Faldo in recent years and James Braid and Bob Jones in the distant past.

Jones was one of many golfers who found that it takes time to appreciate the many subtleties of the Old Course. It has humps and hollows here, there and everywhere; hundreds of bunkers, many in the unlikeliest of places, some such as Hell, Strath, Hill or Road terrifying even the world's greats; huge, rolling greens, all but four of them double greens shared by holes playing in opposite directions; and a wealth of history in every blade of grass – all the greats of golf have played here and the locals will recount tales fantastical of derring-do and catastrophe everywhere on the course. The first-time visitor would be well advised to employ the services of a good local caddie, not only to unravel the mysteries of playing the Old Course but also to share in some of those numerous St Andrews legends.

BOBBY JONES AND ST ANDREWS

Strange to relate, Bobby Jones hated the Old Course on his first visit, tearing up his card during the 1921 Open Championship, but he came to love it as he got to know it better, eventually saying, 'I could take out of my life everything except my experiences at St Andrews and I'd still have a rich, full life.' It was on the Old Course in 1930 that Jones won the Amateur Championship, defeating Roger Wethered 7 and 6. In this remarkable year Jones also won the US Amateur at Merion, the US Open at Interlachen and the Open Championship at Royal Liverpool, a feat unlikely to be repeated, now referred to as the Impregnable Quadrilateral. At the end of that season Jones, at the age of 28, retired from competitive golf, concentrating on his career as a lawyer.

CARD OF THE COURSE

Hole	Distance (yards)	Par
1	376	4
2	453	4
3	397	4
4	480	4
5	568	5
6	412	4
7	390	4
8	175	3
9	352	4
Out	3,603	36
10	380	4
11	174	3
12	348	4
13	465	4
14	618	5
15	456	4
16	423	4
17	455	4
18	357	4
In	3,676	36
Total	7,279	72

LEFT *One of the most famous views in golf, looking over the Swilcan Bridge towards the clubhouse of the R&A.*

BELOW RIGHT *The Road bunker is one of the most feared on the Old Course. Many great players settle for a bogey five rather than risk failing to escape its clutches.*

In the footsteps of the great

There is no simpler drive in golf than that on the 1st hole of the Old Course, or that would be the case if the tee were anywhere else than right in front of the R&A clubhouse. It is a hugely broad fairway shared with the 18th, and there are no bunkers. However, there is the sinuous Swilcan Burn to be cleared to reach the green. Thereafter the course makes its way out in the shape of a shepherd's crook to the Eden Estuary, turning in a loop before retracing its steps alongside the outward holes on wide shared fairways and greens. The space, which appears to invite uninhibited driving and cavalier approach play, is deceptive. Such are the ingenuities of the course's defences that how the hole is played from tee to green depends on exactly where the pin is located.

However much you may be enjoying your round you cannot relax until you have passed the 17th, the Road Hole, dominated by the treacherous Road bunker. Get in there and there may be no escape! But all is surely alleviated by the walk up the 18th, the most famous walk in golf.

'Without a doubt, I like it best of all the Open venues. It is my favourite course in the world.'

TIGER WOODS, OPEN CHAMPION AT
ST ANDREWS IN 2000 AND 2005

BUNKERS – THE STORIES BEHIND THE NAMES

It is said that there are 112 bunkers on the Old Course, which seems a conservative estimate to anyone who has played there. Some of them are in such obscure places that you could never imagine golfers getting into them – but they have! Most also have names. These are some of the more colourful:

CHEAPE'S (2ND HOLE) Named after the Cheape family that owns the nearby Strathtyrum estate. Sir James Cheape bought the Old Course in 1821 to save it from rabbit farmers. His son later sold it to the R&A which, in turn, sold it to the town. Golfers owe Sir James an enormous debt of gratitude.

CARTGATE (3RD HOLE) Shares its name with the hole itself, so called because of the former cart track that crossed the hole towards the beach.

GINGER BEER (4TH HOLE) Again, a name shared with the hole, referring back to the mid-19th century when 'Old Daw' Anderson set up a ginger beer stall there.

SUTHERLAND (4TH/15TH HOLE) Sutherland should not be a factor on the 4th were it not for the difficulties of the right-hand side of the fairway often forcing golfers too far to the left. It was named after one A. G. Sutherland who is reputed to have had the bunker re-excavated when it was filled in in the 1860s.

COTTAGE (4TH/15TH HOLE) For the same reasons as Sutherland, Cottage should not be a factor on the 4th, but it is. It refers to Pilmour Cottage, which once stood nearby and is now the clubhouse of the Eden Course.

STUDENTS (4TH HOLE) There are two theories behind the naming of these bunkers. It has been said that they refer to the practice of busy students, not having the time for a full round, playing out this far and then turning for home. An alternative suggestion is that these were cosy (and out-of-sight) places for male students to take their lady friends.

SPECTACLES (4TH HOLE) This is exactly what they look like, set at the foot of the ridge crossing this fairway.

COFFINS (6TH/13TH HOLES) You are playing a little extravagantly if you get in these on the 6th hole. They are a threat to all, however, on the 13th. They are so coffin-like that you feel you may be in them forever.

SHELL (7TH HOLE) Apart from the fact that it looks rather like a mussel shell from above, the name refers back to the days when the base of the bunker used to be cockle shells. (If you are wildly off course on the 7th, you might find yourself in Hill or Strath bunkers – leave these for the 11th!)

SHORT HOLE BUNKER (8TH HOLE) Some of the bunker names are rather more prosaic!

KRUGER (9TH HOLE) This is actually two bunkers, built during the Boer War and named after the former president of the Transvaal.

A third bunker, further on, is named Mrs Kruger. Rumour has it that there is also one named Kruger's Mistress!

STRATH (11TH HOLE) This commemorates the Strath brothers. Andrew won the 1865 Open Championship. His brother David tied for first place in 1876 but he refused to take part in the play-off, leaving Bob Martin as the champion.

HILL (11TH HOLE) Hill is not far behind Strath in venom. It is cut into the face of the hill on which the 11th green sits.

ADMIRAL'S (12TH HOLE) Sited close to the tee, the bunker is said to have been named after an admiral who, in his 80s, failed to see the sizeable bunker as he walked forward from the tee, distracted as he was by a beautiful young lady walking past, wearing, it is said, pillar-box red.

BELOW *Hell Bunker dominates strategy on the 14th hole for handicap golfers. Will the second shot clear it or do you go round the side of it?*

STROKE (12TH HOLE) Get in here and you almost certainly will drop a stroke.

NICK'S (13TH HOLE) The first of several bunkers threatening a pulled drive, presumably named after the devil who put it there.

CAT'S TRAP (13TH HOLE) Invisible from the fairway, the bunker catches your ball as a cat traps a mouse.

WALKINSHAW (13TH HOLE) Named after a local golfer who made a habit of visiting this pot bunker.

LION'S MOUTH (13TH HOLE) Lion's Mouth is another vicious bunker lying in wait beyond Cat's Trap. Perversely, Lion's Mouth is smaller than Cat's Trap.

THE BEARDIES (14TH HOLE) A quartet of bunkers with whiskery grass adorning their lips.

BENTY (14TH HOLE) Benty refers to one of the traditional seaside grasses: Bent.

KITCHEN (14TH HOLE) Kitchen was once known as the Devil's Kitchen because it was a small but deep pot bunker. It has since been enlarged.

HELL (14TH HOLE) One of the best-known bunkers in golf with a vast acreage and a seriously steep face from which escape forward is by no means guaranteed.

GRAVE (14TH HOLE) A small bunker in front of the green, which was formerly coffin-shaped.

PRINCIPAL'S NOSE (16TH HOLE) A set of three bunkers said to represent the prominent nose of the principal of St Mary's College in the mid-19th century. It is also said to be named after the ugly protuberance from the porch above the doorway of a principal's lodgings in the town.

DEACON SIME (16TH HOLE) Deacon Sime refers to a St Andrews clergyman who asked for his ashes to be scattered in the bunker, on the premise that he had spent so much of his earthly

life in that particular bunker that he might as well spend eternity there as well.

GRANT'S (16TH HOLE) Commemorates a 19th-century captain of the R&A who made a habit of getting into this bunker.

WIG (16TH HOLE) Formerly called Jackson's Wig, recalling the formal dress of golfers in days past. Jackson was a captain of the R&A.

SCHOLAR'S (17TH HOLE) Scholar's is a reminder that the course used to be played in the opposite direction. You were a promising young scholar if you could clear this bunker with your drive.

PROGRESSING (17TH HOLE) You were doing well, but had not yet attained the proficiency of a scholar, if you could clear this bunker.

ROAD (17TH HOLE) The fearsome bunker that eats into the green of the Road Hole, both named after the tarmac road running tight along the right side of the green.

Carnoustie

Carnoustie

Championship Course, Carnoustie Golf Links, Angus, Scotland

Is Carnoustie the toughest course on the Open Championship roster? The way it was prepared for the 1999 Open in the wind and rain it certainly was, Paul Lawrie's winning score being six over par. It was more sympathetically prepared for the 2007 Open, when Padraig Harrington and Sergio Garcia tied on 277, seven under par, Harrington winning in a four-hole play-off. What most observers were agreed on was that this set-up displayed all the greatness of this historic links, and in particular that there were often two or three different strategies for playing a particular hole, depending on a golfer's strengths and weaknesses, the wind and the weather.

It is not certain when golf began in Carnoustie (probably over 500 years ago) but it was some time around 1842 that Allan Robertson – the pre-eminent golfer at that time – was brought from St Andrews to lay out a ten-hole course on the Barry Links. Another St Andrews stalwart, Old Tom Morris, made considerable alterations in 1867, expanding the course to 18 holes, and James Braid made the final significant changes in 1926.

The longest Open Championship course

Carnoustie hosted its first Open Championship in 1931, with Scottish-born American Tommy Armour coming from five behind to win – subsequent champions have included Henry Cotton (1937), Ben Hogan (1953), Gary Player (1963) and Tom Watson (1975). As a championship course Carnoustie has always been among the longest. For the 2007 Open it measured a daunting 7,412 yards/6,778 m, the longest ever, with two par 4s reaching almost 500 yards/457 m in length, yet such is the prowess of contemporary professionals with modern equipment that many forsook their drivers, taking long irons from the tee. They did it for the simple reason that you cannot blast your way round this course. You have to plot your way around it. The bunkers are deep, gathering and perfectly positioned; the rough can be savage; out-of-bounds threatens on several holes; and the Jockie's and Barry burns were brilliantly incorporated into the design, especially on the last two holes.

Jockie's Burn, for instance, limits the length of the tee shot on the challenging 5th, putting pressure on the approach to a multi-level, snaking green, cunningly bunkered and over 50 yards/46 m deep. Out-of-bounds waits to wreck scores on the long 6th, causing many an errant tee shot to be pushed into the deep rough on the other side.

Of all the hazards it is the Barry Burn that is most feared, very largely because it comes into play viciously on the last two holes, hard on the heels of the 16th, a seriously long par 3 on which only the straightest of tee shots can pierce the bunkered mounds guarding the front of the green. Birdies here are rare, dropped shots frequent. The 17th then strikes out over the burn, which meanders hugely, creating almost an island fairway, with length restricted where the burn crosses the fairway.

Still to come is the scariest drive of them all, back over the Barry Burn to another narrow fairway, once again bounded by the burn. Even after a successful drive, there remains the long second to the green, which lies perilously close to the out-of-bounds fence and is, naturally, only just beyond yet another meander of the dreaded burn. What a tough hole!

LEFT *Barry Burn, snaking across the 17th and 18th. Jean van de Velde's skirmishes with it cost him a seven in the 1999 Open Championship, when a six would have won it.*

CARD OF THE COURSE

Hole	Distance (yards)	Par
1	406	4
2	463	4
3	358	4
4	412	4
5	415	4
6	578	5
7	410	4
8	183	3
9	478	4
Out	3,703	36
10	466	4
11	383	4
12	499	4
13	176	3
14	514	5
15	472	4
16	248	3
17	461	4
18	499	4
In	3,718	35
Total	7,421	71

▶ Almost 300 young men from Carnoustie and the surrounding area have emigrated to the United States to work as golf professionals. One of the best known was Stewart Maiden, Bobby Jones's teacher at the East Lake Club, Atlanta.

▶ The Smith brothers from Carnoustie had an enviable professional record. Alex was twice US Open champion, Willie once, and Macdonald came second to Bobby Jones in both the British Open and the US Open in 1930.

▶ Ben Hogan, one of golf's all-time greats, entered only one British Open, in 1953 at Carnoustie. He won the championship by four strokes. It was part of a remarkable run of victories that included the US Masters and the US Open.

'I love playing over here because it allows you to be creative.'
TIGER WOODS

Gleneagles

Gleneagles

King's Course, Gleneagles Hotel, Auchterarder, Perthshire, Scotland

When the 2014 Ryder Cup is played in Scotland it will be at Gleneagles. Jack Nicklaus's PGA Centenary Course has the honour of hosting it, having proved its fitness by hosting the annual Johnnie Walker Championship on the European Tour. The enormous hotel, built in the style of a French château and the venue for the 2005 G8 Summit, will then be exactly 90 years old.

ABOVE The 7th on the King's Course is a tough dogleg on which the further you aim left to shorten the dogleg the longer you have to drive to clear a ridge.

Older still are James Braid's two wonderful courses, opened before the hotel, in 1919. The King's and Queen's courses were a vital part of the strategy to attract royalty, nobility and the merely wealthy to the hotel, the pride and joy of the Caledonian Railway, which was described both as a 'Palace in the Glens' and as the 'Riviera in the Highlands'. Clearly the railway company's ambitions were well founded, for the hotel remains one of the world's great hotels to this day, and Braid's golf courses are as revered as ever.

Both the King's and the Queen's are serious contenders for the coveted title of the finest inland course in Scotland. Neither course is long enough seriously to challenge today's top players – hence the need for the construction of the PGA Centenary Course – but those who value charm, variety, subtlety and ingenuity in a golf course in ravishing surroundings can still derive great satisfaction from a round on either, preferably both. And, of course, they are maintained in impeccable condition.

CARD OF THE COURSE

Hole	Distance (yards)	Par
1	362	4
2	436	4
3	374	4
4	466	4
5	178	3
6	480	5
7	444	4
8	178	3
9	409	4
Out	3,327	35
10	499	5
11	230	3
12	442	4
13	464	4
14	309	4
15	459	4
16	158	3
17	377	4
18	525	5
In	3,463	36
Total	**6,790**	**71**

▶ The principal reason for the wonderful condition of the courses at Gleneagles is that they were built on the sand and gravel left behind when the ice from the Ice Age melted.

▶ 'The finest parcel of land in the world I have ever been given to work with,' is how Jack Nicklaus described the building of the PGA Centenary Course, venue for the 2014 Ryder Cup.

Challenging golf and uplifting scenery

On both courses each hole is named, in keeping with an old Scottish tradition, and at Gleneagles the holes were named from the outset, not carrying forward some ancient traditional name (for the holes were new) but quite simply to amuse visitors. Thus 'Drum Sichty' is no more than a view of the hills while 'Kittle Kink' is a tricky bend. But the names are good ice-breakers between player and caddie, and a good caddie is useful not only in guiding the player through the many problems posed by hilly courses, but also in sharing the finer points of Braid's clever designs with the appreciative golfer.

One of the great delights of the courses is the way the holes follow each other to create an integrated whole, with refreshing changes of pace, a good balance of challenges and a constant sense of development. At a little under 6,000 yards/5,486 m the Queen's Course may seem too short for the accomplished player, but do not be fooled! Seven of the par 4s exceed 400 yards/366 m in length and there are two substantial par 3s, the 14th and 17th. It was a favourite course of Lee Trevino.

In comparison with the Queen's, the King's is said to be more masculine. Sandy Lyle has particular respect for the tough, uphill 4th: in Lyle's opinion, 'a first-class hole by any standard'. Braid himself considered his favourite hole on the course to be the 13th, another long two-shot hole, appropriately named Braid's Brawest ('Braid's Best'). Everywhere there is a sense of space, the twists and turns of each course giving ever-changing views of the uplifting mountain scenery. These are not so much golf courses as experiences!

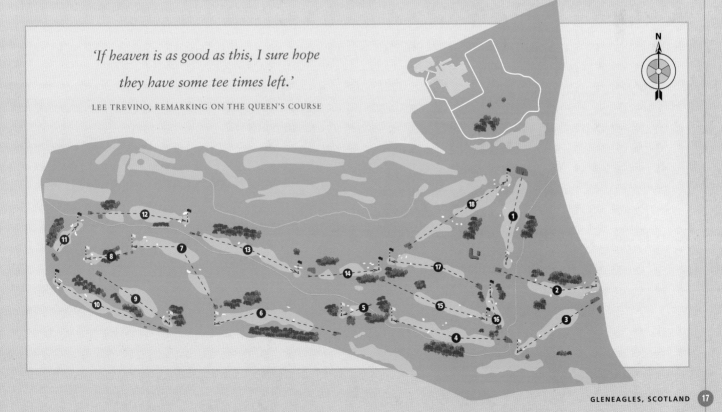

'If heaven is as good as this, I sure hope they have some tee times left.'

LEE TREVINO, REMARKING ON THE QUEEN'S COURSE

Loch Lomond

Loch Lomond Golf Club, Luss by Alexandria, Dunbartonshire, Scotland

Every year, in the week before the Open Championship, eyes turn to Loch Lomond, home of the Scottish Open since 1996. Many of the great names of golf take part in this championship to hone their games for the British Open. To others it represents their last chance to qualify for the big one. For the spectators – and millions who watch on television – it is a rare opportunity to revel in the romantic setting of this very private golf course, set in the historic parkland on the banks of Loch Lomond.

A troubled birth

Loch Lomond was not an instant success. It took years before planning permission was granted and construction could begin. No sooner had ex-Open champion Tom Weiskopf and his design partner, Jay Morrish, completed the course than a recession hit and the receivers were called in. The grass lay fallow. Enter Arizona businessman Lyle Anderson. Weiskopf persuaded him to visit the dormant course. Anderson liked what he saw and agreed to back the venture with cash – lots of it! He now presides over an international club with lavishly appointed facilities, boasting a range of country pursuits, and with two top-class golf courses (the other being Dundonald on the Ayrshire coast).

Eye candy is the bane of much contemporary golf architecture, but at Loch Lomond Weiskopf and Morrish had no need to resort to it. The place is ravishing in its own right and the architects used the mountain and loch vistas superbly, also utilizing the streams and ponds, marshes and woodlands as principal elements in the strategy of design. On the 13th, for instance, there is no sight of the Loch, so a funnel of trees is used to lead the eye from the elevated tee along the well-bunkered fairway of this fine par 5, then beyond up into the heather-clad hills.

This is followed by a great spectator hole, the drivable par-4 14th. The safe play is out to the left, on to a fairway with an iron for position, then a simple pitch over a stream and bunker to the green. The daring play is an all-or-nothing shot over a treacherous bog either on to the green for an eagle putt, or into the bog with a bogey looming.

These are part of a glorious finish, the 17th being a well-defended short hole, and the last hole a strong dogleg where risk-taking is well rewarded, but failure is wretched.

RIGHT There have been three holes-in-one on Loch Lomond's 17th during the Bell's Scottish Open: Jarmo Sandelin and Mathias Grönberg in 2000 and Peter Lonard in 2003.

CARD OF THE COURSE

Hole	Distance (yards)	Par	Hole	Distance (yards)	Par
1	425	4	10	455	4
2	455	4	11	235	3
3	510	5	12	415	4
4	390	4	13	560	5
5	190	3	14	345	4
6	625	5	15	415	4
7	440	4	16	495	4
8	160	3	17	205	3
9	345	4	18	435	4
Out	3,540	36	In	3,560	35
			Total	7,100	71

AN 'AMERICAN COURSE'

There is no such thing as a stereotypical 'American course'. (What have TPC Sawgrass, Merion and Pinehurst in common other than their world fame? Architecturally there is little similarity.) Yet Europe is flooded with 'American-style' courses. Those who golf regularly in the Algarve or Andalucía will instantly recognize one. Loch Lomond is an American-style course – arguably the best in Europe – yet, perversely, it is quite unlike any of the others.

'The opportunity of designing the golf course at Loch Lomond carried with it an awesome sense of responsibility for Jay and me.'

TOM WEISKOPF

Muirfield

Muirfield

The Honourable Company of Edinburgh Golfers, Muirfield, Gullane, East Lothian, Scotland

Muirfield is the third home of the Honourable Company of Edinburgh Golfers, who from 1874 began to host the Open Championship in rotation with Prestwick and St Andrews. In 1891 they moved from Musselburgh to Muirfield, nearly 20 miles/32 km to the east of Edinburgh, calling on Old Tom Morris to lay out their new course.

Only a year after it opened Muirfield hosted its first (and the club's seventh) Open Championship. Fourteen further Opens have followed, as well as the Amateur Championship, Senior Open, Ryder Cup, Walker Cup and Curtis Cup. Some of the greatest names in golf have triumphed at Muirfield, including Vardon, Braid, Hagen, Cotton, Player, Nicklaus, Trevino, Watson, Faldo and Els – an impressive list.

Tom Morris's layout was unusual for its day in consisting of two contra-rotating loops of nine holes, one inside the other. This meant that the wind would blow from a different direction on almost every hole. The routing remains but little else of Morris's course survives, today's being mostly the work of Harry Colt and Tom Simpson in the 1920s.

BELOW *Muirfield's 12th green is slightly raised, with downslopes and bunkers all around, and, as so often on this course, everything is visible as you play your shot.*

THE OLDEST GOLF CLUB

Which is the oldest golf club in the world? Royal Blackheath in southeast London is known to have existed in 1608. Golf was certainly played in Scotland in 1457 because King James II of Scotland issued a decree prohibiting it. It was in the Edinburgh suburb of Leith that the Honourable Company first held a competition over its five-hole course in 1744. As the club's records are complete thereafter, the Honourable Company, which gave the game its first set of rules, becomes the oldest club with a complete, continuous history.

The fairest of tests

The course is well respected by the top players, particularly for its fairness – there is very little blindness and there are few capricious bounces. It is a notably good test of driving, the rough being particularly grasping, and some of its bunkering can only be described as ferocious! Perhaps of all the Open courses Muirfield has no 'stand-out' hole, for it is a very evenly distributed examination of the game, but most players would agree that the 6th, 8th and 18th are among the best long, two-shot holes in links golf. The 13th, too, is a white-knuckle short hole with a long, narrow green perched above five terrifying bunkers. A brilliant escape from one of these set up Ernie Els's Open win in 2002.

From the visitor's point of view, it is worth noting that the club does not introduce temporary tees or winter greens in the off season. You get to play the real course, and for a reduced green fee, to boot.

▶ Jack Nicklaus, after winning the 1966 Open, said, 'It is essentially a fair course. It has more definition than any links that the Open is played on.' He went on to name the first course he created – in Dublin, Ohio, USA – Muirfield Village.

▶ It was at Muirfield, in 1892, that the Open Championship was first played over 72 holes. Previously it had been over 36 holes. It was also at Muirfield in 1892 that an entrance fee to play in the Open Championship was first imposed.

▶ Ben Crenshaw (former US Masters champion and a distinguished golf course architect) praised Muirfield for 'its beautiful honesty as a test of golf'.

CARD OF THE COURSE

Hole	Distance (yards)	Par
1	448	4
2	351	4
3	378	4
4	213	3
5	560	5
6	468	4
7	185	3
8	443	4
9	508	5
Out	3,554	36
10	475	4
11	389	4
12	381	4
13	191	3
14	448	4
15	415	4
16	186	3
17	546	5
18	449	4
In	3,480	35
Total	7,034	71

'I liked it from the first day I played it.'

JACK NICKLAUS, ON WINNING THE 1966 OPEN CHAMPIONSHIP

Royal Dornoch

Royal Dornoch Golf Club, Dornoch, Sutherland, Scotland

'The most fun I ever had playing golf,' was Tom Watson's opinion of Royal Dornoch, an opinion shared by many of the famous golfers who have made the pilgrimage north to Dornoch. They have visited in large numbers because Dornoch is high on the must-play list of all who have an interest in golf course design.

Golf has been played at Dornoch for some 500 years. The present club, with a modest nine-hole course, was founded in 1877 but a more significant date in Dornoch's development was 1883, when John Sutherland was appointed secretary. He it was who brought in Old Tom Morris to extend the course to 18 holes in 1886; who subsequently refined and improved the design; who had the course brought into exemplary condition; who worked to have Dornoch created a Royal club; and who promoted Dornoch in his writings for London periodicals. Sutherland involved his professionals and greenkeepers in the development of the course and one of those was Donald Ross who subsequently emigrated to the United States where he introduced the concept of Dornoch-style raised greens to American golf design.

Remoteness is a blessing for Dornoch

Because Dornoch is so far from large centres of population it has never hosted important professional tournaments or the Open Championship. For that reason the course has been spared the incessant lengthening and alterations that are deemed necessary to keep modern professionals in check. Its holes remain as they were intended to be played twenty, thirty or even fifty years ago and the visitor today is still required to utilize a whole variety of types of pitch shot to gain access to these brilliantly sited greens. But it is not only on the approach shot that intelligent play is demanded, for the fairways use the natural slopes, humps and hollows cleverly, calling for precise and thoughtful driving. The wind, too, must be taken into account.

RIGHT *The delightful 10th hole at Dornoch, a gentle enough par 3 if you find the green from the tee, but the very devil if you miss.*

'It is the most natural course in the world.'

HERBERT WARREN WIND,
THE NEW YORKER

BELOW *A great attraction of Dornoch is the way the course routing takes play into gorse-clad hills, along the sea shore, and over the rolling fairways between.*

CARD OF THE COURSE

Hole	Distance (yards)	Par	Hole	Distance (yards)	Par
1	331	4	10	177	3
2	184	3	11	450	4
3	414	4	12	507	5
4	427	4	13	180	3
5	354	4	14	445	4
6	163	3	15	358	4
7	463	4	16	402	4
8	437	4	17	405	4
9	529	5	18	456	4
Out	3,302	35	In	3,380	35
			Total	6,682	70

Tom Watson's favourite hole is the 5th, a hole that certainly proves that excessive length is not essential for greatness. The view from the elevated tee is encouraging, the wide fairway some way below awaiting the drive. Yet the green is very long and angled significantly from left to right. The ideal drive, then, is down the left, but this is the side where trouble lurks in the form of a hill covered in gorse, threatening a lost ball. On the right the fairway slopes, guiding the ball inexorably towards a run of bunkers. Even if these are avoided the approach shot must be played across the axis of the narrow, kidney-shaped putting surface and there are further bunkers awaiting if that shot is overcooked.

Another of Dornoch's great holes is the bunkerless 14th – Foxy. Everything is governed by a series of dunes, which eat into the fairway from the right, obscuring the green from anywhere other than the extreme left of the fairway. The green is tucked round to the right behind the last of the dunes, broad but shallow, and raised sufficiently to make an approach shot from any length difficult to execute. The 17th, too, is a fine hole, sweeping downhill from the tee, then sharply up to a marvellously located green.

Royal Dornoch

THE LURE OF DORNOCH

John Sutherland, the club's first secretary, was a considerable publicist for Dornoch, writing about it in the *London Daily News* and *Golf Illustrated*. But, unlike many of the great Scottish links that were located near railway lines, Dornoch had no railway until 1902. When the line opened, Sutherland lost no time in alerting golfers to take the overnight sleeper from London, to play the course the following morning. Among those who visited during these years were the Great Triumvirate, James Braid, Harry Vardon and J. H. Taylor. Taylor was so thrilled by the course that he arranged to take a fortnight's holiday in Dornoch every year while he was at the peak of his career, so perfect was the course for honing his game. Another visitor, much later, was Ben Crenshaw, who came to Dornoch as part of his preparations for the 1980 Open Championship, held that year at Muirfield. Asked, when he returned to Muirfield, what he thought of Dornoch he replied, 'Let me put it this way, I nearly did not come back.'

RIGHT *The 2nd at Dornoch looks benign enough from here, but get in the front right bunker and you may well have to escape sideways or backwards.*

Iain Lowe Photography

Royal Troon

Royal Troon Golf Club, Troon, Ayrshire, Scotland

Troon was already an important sea port on the Firth of Clyde when a railway line was opened from Glasgow in 1840. Soon its beaches and clean air attracted Glaswegians to holiday there and the wealthy to build big houses. The next railway station south of Troon was Prestwick, the birthplace of championship golf, and in 1878 it was decided that Troon should have its own golf course.

Land was leased from the Duke of Portland and a five-hole course was created in the area where the present 1st, 2nd, 17th and 18th holes are. That course was extended piecemeal and by 1888 there were 18 holes, stretching to 5,600 yards/ 5,121 m, following much the same route as today's course. Further amendments took place through the years and by 1923 Troon was ready to host its first Open Championship.

Arnold Palmer was at the peak of his career when he won the Open Championship at Troon in 1962, yet even with his extraordinary powers of recovery he realized that he should 'not get locked into a life and death struggle with the course'. The first-time visitor, looking down the opening fairway from the tee, could be forgiven for querying that comment, for everything looks so straightforward and benign. And so it is, for a while.

Increasingly menacing

'As much by skill as by strength' is the club's motto, and the first three holes amble gently alongside the beach, each under 400 yards/366 m in length. Two birdieable par 5s are separated by a charming par 3 on top of the dunes, and everything seems pretty simple so far. The most inviting drive of the round follows at the 7th, but already the mind is sharpening for the mischief of the 8th, the notorious Postage

---

SOCIAL STATUS

At the end of the 1923 Open Championship the champion, Arthur Havers, and runner-up, Walter Hagen, were invited into the clubhouse for the presentation. Hagen refused to go as none of the professional golfers had been admitted to the clubhouse during the tournament. He went instead to the pub where a large number of the spectators joined him.

► At the age of 71 Gene Sarazen played in the 1973 Open Championship at Troon and holed his tee shot on the Postage Stamp for an ace in the first round. In the second round he found a bunker off the tee, but holed his recovery shot.

LEFT *The Postage Stamp was originally played blind to a green on the far side of the dune. The new hole, built in 1909–10, was opened by Harry Vardon, James Braid, J. H. Taylor and Alex Herd.*

CARD OF THE COURSE

Hole	Distance (yards)	Par
1	361	4
2	391	4
3	379	4
4	558	5
5	210	3
6	599	5
7	403	4
8	123	3
9	423	4
Out	3,447	36
10	438	4
11	488	4
12	431	4
13	470	4
14	178	3
15	481	4
16	542	5
17	222	3
18	453	4
In	3,703	35
Total	7,150	71

Stamp. It is the shortest hole in Open Championship golf, but you are either on the minuscule putting surface in one stroke, expecting a birdie, or else, if you missed the green, on a rough-clad hillock, in one of five deep greenside bunkers, or far below the green in a grassy hollow. Escape from any of these is no certainty, as the German player, Hermann Tissies, found to his cost in the 1950 Open. He finished up with a 15!

It is on the back nine, almost invariably played into the wind, that Troon bares its teeth, starting with an intimidating blind and angled drive to the elusive 10th fairway. The subsequent approach to a pinnacle green is difficult to judge. As for the 11th, it was described by Arnold Palmer as, 'The most dangerous hole I have ever seen.' The young Jack Nicklaus ran up a 10 on this hole in his first Troon Open, and during the 1997 Open the hole played to an average of 4.65 shots, easily the hardest on the course. Gorse and the hole's proximity to the railway line are the principal card wreckers.

The corrugated fairways of the 13th and 15th can be difficult to find and hold, the 17th is particularly tough in any sort of wind, and the 18th green is not one to overshoot, with the indignity of out-of-bounds immediately beyond the putting surface.

'The most dangerous hole
I have ever seen.'

ARNOLD PALMER,
DESCRIBING THE 11TH HOLE

Turnberry

Turnberry

Ailsa Course, Westin Turnberry Hotel, Turnberry, Ayrshire, Scotland

Turnberry's Ailsa Course enjoys the most spectacular setting of the half-dozen courses on the Open Championship roster. Often compared to California's Pebble Beach, it made its Open debut in 1977 and immediately produced a classic. Yet twice in its history this most majestic of courses was on the brink of extinction.

The railways played an important part in the spread of golf throughout Britain (America, too, for that matter). They were also responsible for the establishment of some of the country's finest hotels, not least Gleneagles, Cruden Bay and Turnberry. It was in the early 1900s that the Glasgow and South Western Railway negotiated a lease with the Marquis of Ailsa to enable them to construct a hotel at Turnberry. Already in existence on site was the Marquis's private 13-hole course, and a further 13 holes were added so that by 1906

Turnberry could, with justification, call itself a golf resort. It was good enough to host the British Ladies' Championship of 1912, and a promising future seemed certain.

Unfortunately progress was halted by World War I, when the course became an airfield. After that war restoration was undertaken and the thread of development resumed. Worse destruction came in 1939 in the form of a major air base, a vital part of the defence of transatlantic shipping lanes. Surely that was the end for Turnberry.

NAMING OF HOLES

In common with many Scottish courses, Turnberry's holes are named as well as numbered. The 2nd, for instance, is Mak Siccar ('make sure'), the 3rd Blaw Wearie ('out of breath'), 6th Tappie Tourie ('hit to the top'), 10th Dinna Fouter ('don't mess about'), 13th Tickly Tap ('a tricky little hit'), 15th Ca Canny ('take care'), 17th Lang Whang ('good whack').

LEFT *The short 11th, with the lighthouse and Ailsa Craig – the very essence of golf at Turnberry, a scene far removed from the runways of a wartime aerodrome.*

▶ In the final round of the 1979 European Open, played at Turnberry, Sandy Lyle birdied six of the first seven holes to establish an eight-shot lead, going on to win the tournament comfortably. The one hole he failed to birdie was the comparatively simple 2nd.

A remarkable resurrection

It was not the end, however, in the mind of Turnberry's manager, Frank Hole. Despite huge obstacles he managed to garner sufficient compensation from public funds after World War II and enough support from the newly formed British Railways, the hotel's owners, to turn three concrete runways and all their attendant paraphernalia into a fine golf course worthy of the investment. What Scottish designer Philip Mackenzie Ross produced was one of the most visually attractive courses in Britain.

Turnberry then worked its way up the tournament ladder and in 1977 it got its just reward – its first Open. It turned out to be one of the greatest Opens of all, the famous 'duel in the sun', with Tom Watson and Jack Nicklaus going head-to-head to produce some of the most spectacular golf ever seen, Watson just managing to hold out the battling Nicklaus in a thrilling contest.

It could be argued that the first three holes of the Ailsa Course sail under the radar a little, because the player is already anticipating the stretch of shoreline holes from the 4th to the 11th, unparalleled on Open Championship courses and worthy of comparison with those famed seaside holes at Pebble Beach. The seascapes are stunning, especially at sunset, but the golf requires full concentration, with a number of holes threaded down valleys between the dunes, others (such as the short 4th and 6th holes) fully exposed to the wind on top of the dunes. Arguably, the curving 8th is the best of these demanding par 4s, but the visitor cannot wait to be photographed on the peninsular 9th tee, the drive being made over enough of the ocean towards a distant clifftop fairway to cause trepidation in many an otherwise proficient player.

Perhaps the austerities of postwar Britain suggested to Ross a minimalist approach to bunkering, but this aspect was tightened in preparation for the 2009 Open, Turnberry's fourth. The second course, renamed Kintyre, has also been almost wholly remodelled by Donald Steel.

CARD OF THE COURSE

Hole	Distance (yards)	Par
1	350	4
2	430	4
3	462	4
4	165	3
5	442	4
6	231	3
7	529	5
8	431	4
9	454	4
Out	3,494	35
10	452	4
11	174	3
12	446	4
13	412	4
14	449	4
15	209	3
16	409	4
17	497	5
18	434	4
In	3,482	35
Total	6,976	70

The Belfry

Brabazon Course, The Belfry, Warwickshire, England

The Brabazon boasts a unique record – it is the only course on either side of the Atlantic to have hosted four Ryder Cups, with the Europeans winning in 1985 and 2002, the Americans winning in 1993, and the 1989 match halved. It has, then, been a happy hunting ground for the Europeans.

Driving past the courses (there are three) today, all you can see is a fairly unpromising, flat site with lines of parallel trees indicating where fairways might be located. Had you driven past before the courses were built you would not even have seen the trees, for these were potato fields on cold Midlands clay. The property had none of the qualities you would normally look for in assessing its suitability for golf, and golf of the highest class at that.

The job of creating a silk purse out of a sow's ear fell to Peter Alliss and Dave Thomas, and Thomas has returned over the years to make changes and tweaks to allow the course to keep pace with the prodigious advances in performance of golfers, golf clubs and golf balls, particularly over the past twenty years. Alliss and Thomas created a workmanlike course of good length and plenty of challenge on a remarkably modest acreage.

For most of us the strategy of the Brabazon is about avoiding coming to grief in the many streams and lakes that enter into play on almost every hole. There is some prolific bunkering, too, not least on the short 7th, which, from the tee, suggests something out of Pine Valley. Card-wrecking holes come as early as the 3rd, a reachable par 5 (particularly from the everyday tees) with a corner of a lake to be carried on the way to the green, and we might even fall into the pond on the short 12th simply because it is there. But the holes that expose us all (amateur hacker and world star alike) are the 10th and 18th.

Two world-class holes

The 10th is a very short par 4, which actually gets better the shorter it is played. For the Ryder Cup it is reduced from its full 311 yards/284 m to around 270 yards/247 m. The reason is simple: to tempt the contestants to go for the green from the tee. You could get there with two 9-irons. But what would you not give for a putt for an eagle two? Get it wrong, of course, and you are fishing your ball out of the water or you have bounced off the branches of the green-side trees into perdition.

Perhaps the best is kept for last. This is one of the scariest drives in golf, those needing to attack the hole having to clear as much of the lake on the left as they dare. If that is successful, the second shot is played uphill over a further stretch of lake to an enormously long, three-tiered green. All golfers should play this hole once in their lives if only to understand the courage of those Ryder Cup players who have made par or birdie here under monumental pressure.

BELOW *The tough 473-yard (433-m) par-4 18th on the Brabazon Course at the Belfry, one of golf's finest finishing holes, involving two nail-biting crossings of the lake.*

RIGHT *The attractive 10th, a siren hole, luring most golfers into an attempt to drive the green, with the capacity to force most of them to reload – three off the tee!*

CARD OF THE COURSE

Hole	Distance (yards)	Par	Hole	Distance (yards)	Par
1	411	4	10	311	4
2	379	4	11	419	4
3	538	5	12	208	3
4	442	4	13	384	4
5	408	4	14	190	3
6	395	4	15	545	5
7	177	3	16	413	4
8	428	4	17	564	5
9	433	4	18	473	4
Out	3,611	36	In	3,507	36
			Total	7,118	72

Ganton

Ganton

Ganton Golf Club, Scarborough, North Yorkshire, England

If you had to choose a single golf course to encapsulate all that's good about English golf, Ganton would be as good a choice as any. It's old, founded in 1891; it has hosted many high quality tournaments, amateur and professional; it's a mix of heathland and links golf; it's a traditional club yet warmly hospitable; and it's also a great test of all departments of a player's game.

Driving to the course along the busy York–Scarborough road, you could be forgiven for wondering if this were the right road – it just doesn't look like golfing country. Turn down the lane leading to the club and everything changes, even the quality of the air! There are tantalizing glimpses of immaculate fairways and greens, tall pines, cavernous bunkers and hostile gorse. Already it is apparent that only the A game will do.

Ganton is a compact course, which helps to ensure that the pace of play is brisk, although the ingenious routing brings golfers together at different stages of their rounds. Ganton members are sociable, taking every opportunity to compare notes on their respective matches.

INLAND LINKS

What sets the course at Ganton apart from its immediate surroundings is the land on which it was built. This used to be the beach, many thousands of years ago, before the sea retreated to where it is today. Beneath the course is a deep layer of sand giving excellent drainage and supporting the sort of crisp turf more usually encountered at the seaside. Ganton plays like a links, firm and fast. The pitch-and-run shot is usually far more effective than the high-hit wedge, especially in a strong wind, funnelled through the Vale of Pickering.

RIGHT *Ganton's 14th is one of the finest par 4s under 300 yards/274 m in Britain. The setting, in the Vale of Pickering, makes Ganton one of the loveliest places to play.*

▶ Gary Player has said of
Ganton that it is the only inland
course worthy of hosting the
Open Championship – since the
first Open held at Prestwick, the
Open has always been played
on a seaside links.

▶ When Ganton hosted the
1949 Ryder Cup postwar
food rationing was in place.
The American visitors brought
with them 600 steaks, 12
roasting ribs, 12 hams and
12 boxes of bacon. They won!

On the course

The prospect from the 1st tee is inviting, a welcoming fairway rising gently in front of you, before sliding to the right past bunkers to a green, bunkered on either side of the entrance. It is not a difficult hole, but you are immediately aware that sloppy play will not go unpunished. Again, it is the bunkering that keeps you on your toes on the 2nd, and bunkering provides a stiff challenge for those aspiring to drive the 3rd green. From here the course twists and turns over a sequence of delightful holes, meeting the wind from every angle, until on the 14th the course bares its teeth. It may be a short par 4, but it is a brilliant one, tempting bold play and cruelly punishing the inadequate.

Strong hitting is needed to conquer the 15th, and it will be useful on the 16th tee where you are required to clear a monumental quarry of a bunker in mid-fairway. The harder task is positioning the drive correctly to grant an unimpeded approach to the green, raised above bunkers and backed by bright yellow gorse. The 17th is a brutal long short hole (played as a par 4 by visitors), and the round ends with a supremely strategic dogleg. Greed will bring disaster! Then it's time for a drink and a slice of the famous Ganton cake.

CARD OF THE COURSE

Hole	Distance (yards)	Par	Hole	Distance (yards)	Par
1	373	4	10	168	3
2	445	4	11	417	4
3	334	4	12	363	4
4	406	4	13	524	5
5	157	3	14	282	4
6	470	4	15	461	4
7	435	4	16	448	4
8	414	4	17	249	3
9	504	5	18	434	4
Out	3,538	36	In	3,346	35
			Total	6,884	71

Royal Birkdale

Royal Birkdale

Royal Birkdale Golf Club, Southport, Merseyside, England

There is refreshingly little pomp for a club and course with such history. The respect of being chosen for the 100th Open Championship and a consistent ranking in the UK Top 10 are quite sufficient for Royal Birkdale.

A striking sight greets visitors to Royal Birkdale: a white art-deco clubhouse resembling a ship sailing on a tossing sea of sand dunes. It was designed in 1935 to replicate the superstructure of the ocean liners that in those days steamed out from Liverpool in considerable numbers, heading for all corners of the then intact British Empire. Within the clubhouse, however, its creature comforts most definitely belong to the 21st century.

True links golf is played in partnership with nature, and Birkdale's course uses little trickery or human intervention to create its challenges, the difficulties coming instead with subtle design and substantial yardages. Thick rough and willow scrub devour errant shots, and act as a wonderful haven for a wide variety of wildlife. However, the design (evolved over the years by the Hawtree family of golf course architects) is actually very simple: holes weave through valleys between sand hills, creating flat fairways (for a links!)

giving the reward of many yards of roll on a well-struck shot, and a good stance for the next shot. The crests and troughs of that tossing sea of sand dunes are omnipresent, but you are only troubled by them if you stray off line. There are some fine tee and green sites high on them, such as the 11th tee and 12th green.

A long and distinguished championship history

Host to the Open Championship on nine occasions between 1954 and 2008, Royal Birkdale always proves to be an outstanding venue, with its fair nature rewarding good play, while the sand hills lining the fairways create a set of natural grandstands for spectators, the best of any course on the Open roster. The overriding feedback from every Open is that the course is hard but fair, and it is a consistent favourite with the professionals.

The rough can be brutal for Open week. In 1971 Lee Trevino joked: '… at 15 we put down my bag to hunt for a ball, found the ball, lost the bag!'

LEFT *Overlooking the final green, Royal Birkdale's unique clubhouse resembles an ocean liner, so many of which used to steam past the course on their way out from Liverpool.*

A PROUD MOMENT FOR GOLF

One of golf's great gentlemen, Jack Nicklaus generously conceded a short but missable putt to Tony Jacklin on the 18th green at the climax of the 1969 Ryder Cup at Birkdale, a putt that allowed the home team to tie with the Americans. 'I am sure you would have holed, but I was not prepared to see you miss,' was Nicklaus's brotherly remark to his opponent.

The difficult 1st, a long, left-hand dogleg, sets the precedent that accurate hitting is key, with out-of-bounds right, the infamous 'Jutland' bunker on the left, and characteristic mounds that block approaches to the green from poor positions. Although trees are never a factor in regulation play, they often provide a handsome backdrop, such as when they top the dunes behind the 2nd green, a green cunningly contoured and guarded by pot bunkers.

As with all good designs, planning from the tee is essential to allow the correct approach shot to the green, such as on the tough 6th, on which one must flirt with a huge bunker on the right to leave a decent angle to the elevated green. The holes twist and turn through the dunes allowing the prevailing wind to hit from every angle.

There is good variation to the holes, with short par 4s such as the dogleg 5th and downhill 11th both requiring good management. The greens, which were completely rebuilt by Martin Hawtree in the 1990s, are a fine test, with mounds, hollows and clever bunkering around them calling for an imaginative short game, summed up by Seve Ballesteros's famous chip-and-run between the bunkers on the 18th in 1976.

CARD OF THE COURSE

Hole	Distance (yards)	Par
1	449	4
2	421	4
3	407	4
4	203	3
5	344	4
6	480	4
7	177	3
8	457	4
9	411	4
Out	3,349	34
10	403	4
11	408	4
12	183	3
13	498	4
14	198	3
15	544	5
16	416	4
17	547	5
18	472	4
In	3,669	36
Total	7,018	70

Royal Liverpool

Royal Liverpool

Royal Liverpool Golf Club, Hoylake, Wirral, England

Founded in 1869, Royal Liverpool (or Hoylake as it is popularly known) is one of England's oldest golf clubs. Golf was first played here alongside amateur horse and pony races, for this was the site of the Liverpool Hunt Club. Naturally, the horses were not expected to charge up and down the sand dunes, so, for the most part, this is an unusually flat course. But appearances can be deceptive, especially here.

In no time at all (1872) Hoylake had attracted its first professional tournament – in fact the first of any significance outside Scotland. The first prize was almost double the prize for the Open Championship. It attracted a small but distinguished field with Young Tom Morris emerging victorious. Next up was the inaugural Amateur Championship (1885), followed by its first Open Championship (1897). The winner on this occasion was Royal Liverpool's own Harold Hilton; he and his club companion John Ball were the only amateurs to win the Open Championship until the emergence of Bobby Jones, who won at Hoylake in 1930. This was to become the second leg of his incredible 'Impregnable Quadrilateral', when he won the Open and Amateur Championships of the United States and Britain in the same year. The Open returned to Hoylake several times, but after Roberto de Vicenzo's victory in 1967 there was a lengthy gap until 2006, when Tiger Woods showed everybody else how to play the course.

RIGHT *The 12th green presents a difficult target, raised up on top of the dunes, but it gives wonderful views over the Dee Estuary to the Flintshire hills.*

Woods – the great strategist

As he had done previously at St Andrews in 2005, Woods analysed the course from the point of view of his own strengths, deciding that it was too dangerous to use the driver prospectively from the tee. He reckoned that if he played for position rather than length, making sure that his tee shot landed in the best spot from which to approach the green, his long-iron play to the green would get him close to the hole. His approach play that week was imperious.

The order of the holes was altered for the Open, but more usually Hoylake begins with a unique hole, a bunkerless par 4 on which it is possible to drive out of bounds on either side. The green adjoins a 'cop' (a grassy bank, typical of Hoylake) which is also out of bounds. Like the first hole, most of the early holes are level, but there is a relentlessness about the probing that never lets up. The wind rarely lets up either.

As the round progresses the character of the course changes gradually until the 8th, when the pitch is made steeply uphill to a rolling green standing on top of the dunes, giving way to a glorious sequence of seaside holes with expansive views. The pick of these must be the 12th, a majestic par 4 beginning with a drive to a low, curving fairway, followed by a long second shot uphill to a brilliantly sited green, repelling all but the finest approaches. Woods solved its problems on the second day of the Open by pitching in for an eagle. His approach, stone dead, on the final afternoon was breathtaking. Great golf on a great course!

▶ For the 2006 Open Championship a number of alterations were made to the course, including a brand new 17th hole (played as the 1st for the championship). The old green was so near to a road that it was not unknown for players to putt out of bounds.

CARD OF THE COURSE

Hole	Distance (yards)	Par
1	429	4
2	372	4
3	528	5
4	202	3
5	453	4
6	423	4
7	198	3
8	534	5
9	393	4
Out	3,532	36
10	448	4
11	198	3
12	456	4
13	161	3
14	554	5
15	459	4
16	560	5
17	454	4
18	436	4
In	3,726	36
Total	7,258	72

'I know no better golf course anywhere in the world.'

BERNARD DARWIN

▶ The 6th hole is unusual among championship courses in that the drive is made over the corner of an orchard.

Wentworth

Wentworth

West Course, Wentworth Club, Virginia Water, Surrey, England

Driving through the vast Wentworth Estate is a voyage of discovery. The mansions of the rich and famous line the lanes and drives, many of them backing on to the fairways of the three golf courses that occasionally cross the roads, causing the driver to stop while a four-ball launches its tee shots on their journeys.

ABOVE *Wentworth's West Course is as visually attractive as it is demanding. It is one of those courses that invites you to play good shots. This is the par-3 2nd.*

The Wentworth Estate came into being in the 1920s through the vision, entrepreneurial skills and extraordinary confidence of a developer – George Tarrant. When it came to constructing the golf courses, Tarrant knew exactly who to use – Harry Colt. Colt and Tarrant had collaborated on a similar scheme some years earlier at St George's Hill, and the success of both ventures has ensured that both are among the most desirable places to live in the whole London area.

Colt built the East Course in 1924. Today it measures only a little over 6,000 yards/5,486 m, but it is a thoroughly entertaining course and was good enough to host a match between the professionals of America and Great Britain and Ireland in 1926, thus paving the way for the Ryder Cup. The East was also the venue for the inaugural Curtis Cup, between women amateur golfers of the United States and Great Britain and Ireland, in 1932. Second up was the West Course, also Colt-designed, of 1926. There was then a gap of over 60 years until the third course, the Edinburgh, opened in 1990. This was designed by John Jacobs in association with Gary Player and Bernard Gallagher.

The Burma Road

When it opened, the West Course was found to be long and hard, tough enough for it to be dubbed the Burma Road. Its length is not so fearsome today but the name has stuck and twice a year television audiences get to see it in fine condition, hosting the PGA Championship in the spring and the World Matchplay in the autumn. Recent adjustments to the course by Ernie Els (who lives on the estate) have pushed the overall length up from just over 7,000 yards/6,400 m to more than 7,300 yards/6,675 m. Visitors playing it from the yellow tees still find it quite long enough at over 6,700 yards/6,125 m.

Length is not everything, however, and some of the best holes are modest on paper. The delightful 154-yard/141-m 2nd, for instance, is played from a high tee across a road to an elusive ledge green. The 6th, 7th and 8th are each among the shorter par 4s, but their greens are notoriously hard to locate. The short 14th is played uphill to a multi-level green, the hill being steep enough to deceive the eye, and club selection further complicated if there is a wind. Similarly, the 16th regularly sets problems for the professionals under tournament conditions.

A new tee has been found for the 17th, stretching it to a monstrous – and treacherous – 610 yards/558 m. It is all too easy to drive out of bounds on the left, so the natural reaction is to err to the right, increasing the length of the hole and very probably resulting in a clinging lie, or even finishing behind a tree. Nor is the green easy to find, on high ground, the fairway constantly curving. The Els-modified 18th is now a particularly strong finishing hole.

▶ In addition to the PGA Championship and World Matchplay, the West Course has hosted the Ryder Cup (1953) and the Canada Cup (1956), when Ben Hogan made one of his all-too-rare visits to the UK, winning the tournament with Sam Snead as partner.

CARD OF THE COURSE

Hole	Distance (yards)	Par
1	473	5
2	154	3
3	465	4
4	552	5
5	212	3
6	418	4
7	396	4
8	401	4
9	452	4
Out	3,523	36
10	184	3
11	416	4
12	531	5
13	470	4
14	179	3
15	490	4
16	383	4
17	610	5
18	538	5
In	3,801	37
Total	7,324	73

Woodhall Spa

Hotchkin Course, Woodhall Spa, Lincolnshire, England

Of all Britain's great courses the Hotchkin Course at Woodhall Spa must be the least known – for the very simple reason that it lies in a remote corner of the country, not really on the way to or from anywhere. Despite its inviting title, Woodhall Spa is little more than a charming village, but it has had a golf course since 1890.

The club had rather a troubled history, and the local landowner, Stafford Vere Hotchkin, repeatedly came to the rescue, first by writing off the club's rent arrears and in 1919 by buying the club. After a succession of moves and different course layouts, the club was lucky enough to possess, by this time, a fine Harry Colt course laid out on a rare tract of sandy heath. But Hotchkin was not merely a financial benefactor, he was also a more than competent golfer and a course designer himself. Between 1919 and his death in 1953 he made a large number of refinements to the design, turning the course into one of England's most demanding. Hotchkin's son Neil continued to run the club after his father's death, which ensured that the design was not tampered with and Hotchkin's ethos maintained. In 1995 he sold the course to the English Golf Union (EGU), who made their headquarters there, bringing in Donald Steel to build a second – and utterly different – course (the Bracken), while keeping Hotchkin's course in the manner of which he would have approved.

RIGHT *The bunkering at Woodhall Spa is among the most formidable in Britain. It is deep, steep-faced and prolific. This is the 5th green, surrounded by sand.*

▶ One of Hotchkin's principles of golf course design was: 'The best results are obtained by making a course conform to the natural surroundings that already exist, so that it will not look artificial and fail to blend with the landscape.' Woodhall Spa is a shining example.

▶ Because of its location Woodhall Spa has staged few professional tournaments, but it has featured prominently in the amateur calendar, hosting such tournaments as the English Amateur, Brabazon Trophy, St Andrews Trophy and Ladies' British Open Amateur.

N

▶ During a club match in 1982 a member holed the 12th in one – as, then, did his opponent, for the half!

CARD OF THE COURSE

Hole	Distance (yards)	Par	Hole	Distance (yards)	Par
1	361	4	10	338	4
2	442	4	11	437	4
3	415	4	12	172	3
4	414	4	13	451	4
5	148	3	14	521	5
6	526	5	15	321	4
7	470	4	16	395	4
8	209	3	17	336	4
9	584	5	18	540	5
Out	3,569	36	In	3,511	37
			Total	7,080	73

England's most frightening bunkers?

Until you have played Woodhall Spa it is difficult to imagine just how ferocious its bunkers are. It is a moot point whether Ganton or Woodhall Spa has the most savage bunkering in England. Ganton's are more visible and perhaps more frightening to the eye. Woodhall Spa's bunkers are deeper – sinister trenches very often topped off with eyebrows of heather – and sometimes invisible from a distance. A bunker may be as deep as the height of a man. In some cases these are set tight against elevated greens and you may have to raise the ball 10 feet/ 3 m vertically to gain the safety of the putting surface. The strange thing is that Ganton and Woodhall Spa are such lovely courses that, however roughly they may treat you, you still enjoy the experience immensely.

Woodhall Spa charms you from the outset, with a delicate, short two-shot hole to get play under way. You could be lulled into a false sense of security, but on the 2nd hole the course bares its teeth, with the deepest of bunkers threatening the drive of all lengths of hitters, and the green has a narrow entrance. And if a bunker does not get you the heather most surely will. It may look lovely, but a rash shot out of it may result in a broken wrist.

What makes Woodhall Spa so enticing is the wonderful variety of the holes, with no two the same. There are great long two-shotters, but it may be the collection of par 3s (only three of them) that remain in the memory longest.

Woodhall Spa

IN TUNE WITH NATURE

The Hotchkin Course occupies a valuable piece of heathland, a habitat that is disappearing all too quickly in Britain. It has, therefore, been designated as a Site of Special Scientific Interest. The National Golf Centre, headquarters of the EGU, works in partnership with Natural England to manage the land to help preserve its biodiversity. It is an ongoing project and will, in time, restore more of the original heathland, removing plants and trees that are not natural to the heath. At the same time, long-lost bunkers and other features from the earlier courses are being discovered and brought back into action.

RIGHT *There is a timeless quality to golf at Woodhall Spa, a sense of getting away from it all, and this old ruined tower recalls an age long before golf.*

Celtic Manor

Celtic Manor

Twenty Ten Course, Celtic Manor Resort, Newport, Wales

The golf courses at Celtic Manor, host to the Ryder Cup in 2010, are contemporary in every way, but the ground over which they run is steeped in ancient history. They overlook the remains of the Roman town of Caerleon and, running from it, the Via Julia was an important communication route connecting this Welsh outpost to the Roman settlements in England. Its remains cross the Celtic Manor estate.

In the 5th century the lands were acquired by the Bishops of Llandaff and in the 17th century a manor house was built for the local high sheriff. But the estate as it now is first took shape in the 1860s when the enormously prosperous industrialist, Thomas Powell, had Coldra House built for his son. Subsequently the house became a maternity hospital. It closed in 1975 and was in danger of falling into ruin until a wealthy businessman, Sir Terry Matthews, bought it in 1981, restoring it for use initially as a small luxury hotel. Since then the story has been one of considerable expansion. The hotel can now accommodate almost 2,000 conference delegates and in 1995 golf arrived on the scene in the shape of the Roman Road Course, which, as its name suggests, keeps close company with the Via Julia.

The Roman Road Course was designed by one of the legends of golf course design, Robert Trent Jones, who in his 70-year career built over 300 courses, including the Ryder Cup venue, Valderrama, in Spain, and made alterations to a further 150. Jones returned to Celtic Manor to build a short course, Coldra Woods, and later to team up with his son, Robert Jr, to lay out the enormously long Wentwood Hills Course – an extraordinary mix of alpine holes and others that might have been lifted bodily from Florida, with the obligatory lakes to the fore in the lowland section.

Bold decisions

Matthews was ambitious for his resort. He wanted to attract the biggest stars in the game to play there and he set out to bring the Ryder Cup to Wales for the first time. His problem was that none of his existing courses could accommodate such a tournament. Roman Road was not tough enough and Wentwood Hills was spectator-unfriendly, with an exhausting hill climb required on the back nine. Drastic measures were needed, and Matthews was not afraid to take bold decisions.

The boldest decision was to abandon the Wentwood Hills Course, considered the jewel in the crown of the resort. It has not been wasted, for the upland holes have been incorporated in a new course designed by Colin Montgomerie, and nine of the low-lying holes have been retained as part of the course specifically designed to attract the Ryder Cup, lying entirely in the Usk Valley. Matthews's brave move was successful, and the Ryder Cup matches will be played in Wales for the first time in 2010, on this course now known as the Twenty Ten.

As might be expected, it is a heroic course playing to almost 7,500 yards/6,858 m from the back tees. For those matches that make it to the par-5 18th hole – one of three par 5s over 600 yards/(549 m – there remains a death-or-glory gamble on whether to try to reach the green in two across a green-front lake. Roman gladiators would have understood the pressures; Ryder Cup spectators will relish the contest.

▶ Thomas Powell, founder of the Powell-Duffryn Company and the world's first millionaire, employed 13,500 workers in his coal business, 11,600 of them working underground.

LEFT *The tranquillity of the Usk Valley will become a cauldron of high emotion when the Ryder Cup matches are played at Celtic Manor. This is the 14th.*

CARD OF THE COURSE

Hole	Distance (yards)	Par
1	465	4
2	610	5
3	189	3
4	461	4
5	457	4
6	452	4
7	213	3
8	439	4
9	666	5
Out	3,952	36
10	210	3
11	562	5
12	458	4
13	189	3
14	413	4
15	377	4
16	508	4
17	211	3
18	613	5
In	3,541	35
Total	7,493	71

'There's water, drivable par 4s and the finishing stretch is fantastic.'

IAN WOOSNAM,
CAPTAIN OF EUROPEAN
TEAM, 2006 RYDER CUP

Royal County Down

Royal County Down

Royal County Down Golf Club, Newcastle, County Down, Northern Ireland

On the coast of Dundrum Bay, backed by the Mourne Mountains, 18 holes weave purposefully through dunes and gorse to create, in the words of Tom Watson, 'a pure links'. For over 100 years, Old Tom Morris's routing has changed little, and as such there is a sense that the course has always been here, quietly tucked away in this beautifully unassuming place.

Don't be mistaken in assuming that the age and tradition of the course have left it obsolete in today's game. Though quite capable of hosting major tournaments, Royal County Down has opted to avoid these events, fearing that the course and indigenous wildlife would suffer from trampling spectators and media villages – the Senior British Open and Walker Cup are the biggest events of recent times. It is especially impressive, therefore, that many great players have made the pilgrimage to this wonderful course simply to experience it. Famously, Tiger Woods has chosen these holes to sharpen his links skills before an Open Championship.

A perfect nine?

The front nine is commonly regarded as the best front nine in golf (not to say that the back nine is shabby). A great starting hole, the par-5 1st is reachable in two, but one must carry the ball long down the left-hand side to take advantage of the sloping fairway, which bounds the ball forwards towards the green. As poor drives are punished, with dunes on both sides and the beach on the right, this hole sets the precedent that control is a necessity. Another somewhat daunting feature during the round is that of playing tee shots over dunes, blind or semi-blind.

After the first couple of drives, which play in the same direction over intimidating hills, when guests reach the 4th tee members often allow them to set up with driver aiming over the dune before pointing out that this is a par 3 played in the opposite direction! Looking in the correct direction from this elevated tee, one is blessed by a gorgeous view of the mountains and sea, but the player can also see the countless challenges ahead. After a carry over gorse bushes, nine brutish bunkers surround a green with large drop-offs to both sides and the back.

Possibly the best hole on the back nine is the 13th. Bunkers plague the dogleg on the right-hand side, and a decent hit down the left is rewarded with lengthy run on the mounds of the firm fairway. If the drive is too short, sight of the green is blocked by the gorse-banked dune on the dogleg. The broad, sloping green is nestled among dunes to create its own amphitheatre, backed by swathes of lilac heather. The strength of holes like this, coupled with picturesque scenery and legendary hospitality, have led Royal County Down to a consistent ranking as one of the world's Top 10 courses.

LEFT *Slieve Donard, the highest of the Mourne Mountains, overlooks Dundrum Bay and the historic Royal County Down links. This is the excellent 3rd hole, viewed from behind the green.*

▶ In 1933, in the Irish Open Amateur Championship, Eric Fiddian recorded two holes-in-one in the final, yet still lost.

CARD OF THE COURSE

Hole	Distance (yards)	Par
1	539	5
2	444	4
3	477	4
4	213	3
5	440	4
6	398	4
7	145	3
8	430	4
9	486	4
Out	3,572	35
10	197	3
11	440	4
12	527	5
13	444	4
14	212	3
15	467	4
16	337	4
17	435	4
18	550	5
In	3,609	36
Total	7,181	71

BELOW *The bunkers at Royal County Down are serious, both in expanse and depth. Many are topped off by eyebrows of heather or clinging rough grass. These threaten the drive at the 8th.*

'*For visual splendour and golf on a heroic scale, there is nothing better.*'

DONALD STEEL, *CLASSIC GOLF LINKS OF GREAT BRITAIN AND IRELAND*

Royal Portrush

Royal Portrush

Dunluce Links, Royal Portrush Golf Club, County Antrim,
Northern Ireland

The Dunluce course at Portrush is the only course outside Great Britain to have staged the Open Championship, which it did once, in 1951, with the dapper Max Faulkner emerging victorious. There is little doubt that the course could still examine the world's best, but the infrastructure of this beautiful corner of Northern Ireland simply could not cope with the huge numbers of visitors, golfers, spectators and the media that a modern Open Championship brings.

Royal Portrush is an old club, founded as the County Club in 1888, but its two fine courses (the other being the Valley course) owe their distinction to Harry Colt, who rebuilt and re-routed Old Tom Morris's original course in 1932. What Colt did was golf architecture at its simplest. He noted the parallel lines of sand dunes and routed the holes along the defining valleys between them. His genius, however, was to choose the optimum locations for tees and greens. Indeed, these greens are some of the most testing to find in top-class links golf, despite their having a mere handful of bunkers

guarding them. As a result of Colt's cunning use of the shapes of the dunes, none of the par 4s and 5s from the 2nd to the 16th is straight. They all bend one way or another. Dunluce Links is, then, one of the most demanding driving courses in British golf.

A mounting sense of expectation

Even before you reach the course anticipation is eager, the twisting road running along the magnificent rocky coast of County Antrim, past the Giant's Causeway and the ruins of

RIGHT *Colt took full advantage of the nature of the ground at Portrush to create brilliantly sited (and defended) greens, such as the 13th. The Dunluce needs, therefore, fewer bunkers than most other comparable courses.*

Dunluce Castle. Suddenly, round a bend, you espy the courses for the first time, and the sight is thrilling. Even the most experienced links golfer cannot fail to be excited by the tumbling nature of the ground and the broad seascape.

The course, too, builds over the first few holes, until on the 5th tee you stand overlooking a distant fairway angled away to the right towards a green located on the very edge of the Atlantic Ocean. Visually, it is a stunning hole, but already the screw is being turned. That hole had no need of bunkers, nor do two of the best short holes, the 6th and 14th. A full carry over inhospitable low ground is required to reach the plateau green of the 6th, the hole that carries the name of its architect, Harry Colt.

Calamity is the name of the 14th, probably the most famous hole at Portrush. It is an appropriate name if you come up short or, worse, down in the abyss on the right – woe betide those plagued by a slice. This hole is perhaps as near as you can get to a dogleg par 3! You have to aim left and allow the ground in front of the green to feed the ball to the right. A good, traditional ground-game shot is what is required here, and at a little over 200 yards/183 m a sound technique is demanded. Foozling does not work at Portrush!

The Senior British Open Championship was held at Royal Portrush in 1995. It was won by Brian Barnes, the son-in-law of Max Faulkner, winner of the Open Championship on the same course in 1951.

Inspired by a new putter, Max Faulkner led the field after the second round and was flamboyantly signing autographs 'Open Champion 1951'. Despite tempting fate so extravagantly, he did indeed go on to win.

CARD OF THE COURSE

Hole	Distance (yards)	Par	Hole	Distance (yards)	Par
1	392	4	10	478	5
2	505	5	11	170	3
3	155	3	12	392	4
4	457	4	13	386	4
5	384	4	14	210	3
6	189	3	15	365	4
7	431	4	16	428	4
8	384	4	17	548	5
9	475	5	18	469	4
Out	3,372	36	In	3,446	36
			Total	6,818	72

'Portrush is flying golf – one longs to take off after the ball.'

PATRIC DICKINSON,
A ROUND OF GOLF COURSES

Ballybunion

Ballybunion

The Old Course, Ballybunion, County Kerry, Republic of Ireland

A round of golf on the Old Course at Ballybunion is a unique experience. None other than Tom Watson would agree. He was very much responsible for alerting the world to the existence of this extraordinary place, which was largely unknown outside Ireland when he first visited in 1981. Now acknowledged as one of the world's greatest courses, many a star golfer has made the pilgrimage to play it.

Ballybunion is a long-established club, founded in 1893 in the far west of Ireland on a stretch of quite incomparable dunes overlooking the Atlantic Ocean. There are many golf courses in the west of Ireland set on dunes overlooking the Atlantic, but what sets Ballybunion apart is the way the course is routed over, through, across and along the dunes. So the golfer is asked to play a huge catalogue of different shots throughout the round to adapt to the constantly changing topography.

BELOW *The full might, majesty, dominion and power of Ballybunion as portrayed by the conjunction of the wonderfully sited 10th green and beyond it the magical 11th fairway.*

COASTAL EROSION

It is the stuff of nightmares – seeing your course washed away by the unstoppable power of the sea. The venerable Olympic Club in San Francisco lost a number of holes to the Pacific Ocean some years ago. Ballybunion, too, faced the prospect of losing some of its finest holes to the Atlantic Ocean in the 1970s. An appeal was launched, and that was when Ballybunion found that it had friends, generous ones, all over the world. With the threat of global warming raising sea levels erosion is on many clubs' agendas throughout the world.

Natural hazards

The Old Course excites golfers of all abilities. The round starts ominously, for there is a graveyard awaiting the merest slice from the 1st tee, and from here to the corner of the dogleg on the 6th the course slides into gear rather as an Irish morning slowly gathers momentum. At this point the adrenaline kicks in, with a delicious pitch up to a green on top of the dunes, the first of a series of greens that seriously tests every department of the approach game. This hole has no need of a bunker and, once away from the opening (inland) holes, there are remarkably few bunkers on the course as a whole. Such is the brilliance of the green sites that grassy swales and fall-aways protect the holes even more strongly than sand would.

Indeed, one of the finest holes on the course – one of the world's great holes – has no bunker, either. It is the unforgettable 11th, a gorgeous hole tumbling down through the sand hills alongside the Atlantic with a green cleverly defended by encircling dunes. There are great holes still to come, but it was the short 8th that particularly appealed to Watson on his first visit, with an all-or-nothing shot to a tiny green and desperate recovery work required should the tee shot fail to hold the putting surface.

Ballybunion boasts back-to-back par 3s on the inward half, the 14th and 15th. Like every hole here, they were dictated naturally by the exciting land forms, and the 15th is a great short hole, played to a marvellous green backed by the Atlantic Ocean. Then the excellent 16th and 17th both make excursions to the oceanside. Ballybunion should be on every golfer's must-play list.

▶ Ballybunion was enlarged into an 18-hole course in 1926. The 'designer' was a Mr Smyth. His layout was so good that when Tom Simpson was engaged to upgrade it in 1937 he suggested only three minor changes.

▶ Ballybunion is so far from any major population centre that it has hosted the Irish Open only once, in 2000. Sweden's Patrik Sjöland emerged victorious after opening rounds of 64 and 65.

CARD OF THE COURSE

Hole	Distance (yards)	Par
1	392	4
2	445	4
3	220	3
4	498	5
5	508	5
6	364	4
7	423	4
8	153	3
9	454	4
Out	3,457	36
10	359	4
11	449	4
12	192	3
13	484	5
14	131	3
15	216	3
16	490	5
17	385	4
18	379	4
In	3,085	35
Total	6,542	71

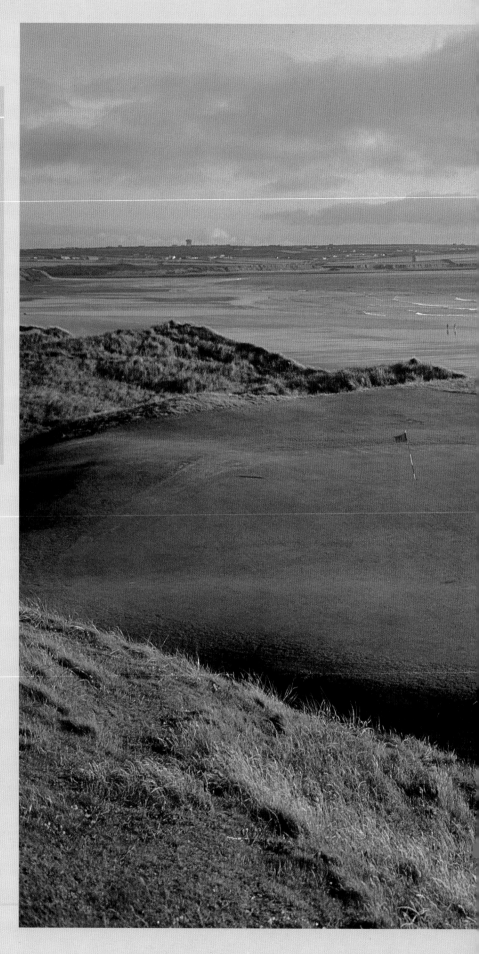

Ballybunion

FINEST PIECE OF LINKSLAND

In the late 1960s the decision was taken to purchase further duneland to the south of the existing links. By 1980 sufficient funds had been raised to consider building a second course and Robert Trent Jones was approached. He wrote, 'I was given both a once-in-a-lifetime opportunity and a terrifying challenge . . . the property I had to work with is perhaps the finest piece of linksland in the world.' In 1984 the Cashen Course was completed but it is proving to be controversial. Jones made spectacular use of the site, but the course is too hard for higher-handicap players. That said, the Cashen possesses a fabulous collection of green sites and Ballybunion as a whole offers a wonderful test of approach work.

RIGHT *Tom Watson rated the 11th as 'one of the toughest holes in the world . . . a small target with not a lot of room to miss right or left.'*

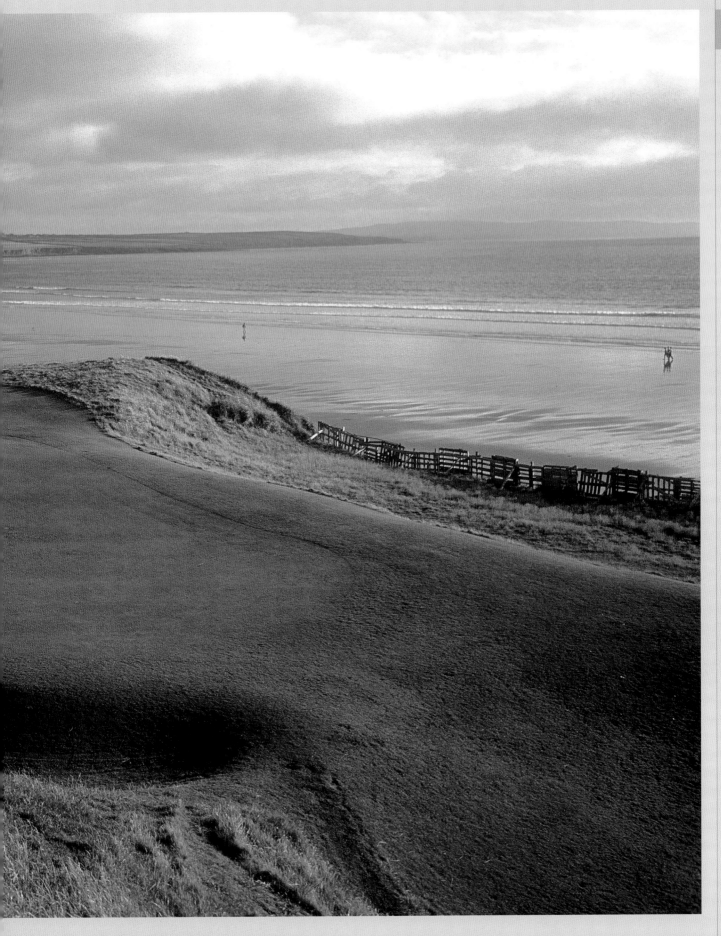

The K Club

The K Club, Straffan, County Kildare, Republic of Ireland

With Irish golf going from strength to strength in recent years, the K Club was a fitting venue for the 2006 Ryder Cup. Roared on by hoards of supporters, the golf was often inspired, not least Scott Verplank's hole-in-one on the 14th. But it was Europe who came to the fore, eventually equalling the record-winning margin of 18½ to 9½. The K Club will be remembered for these emotional scenes for many years to come.

Although most of the golf played at the K Club is medal or resort play, the course seems particularly suited to matchplay events. The majority of matches finish on the 16th and 17th holes and the Arnold Palmer design is strong at this point. It should be added that for professional tournaments the holes are played in a different order from the day-to-day routing. So what is normally the 7th plays as the 16th during events such as the Ryder Cup. Interestingly, on such occasions the length is reduced from a possible 600 yards/549 m to something around 570 yards/521 m or less in order to encourage players to go for the green in two, requiring a daring shot across the River Liffey. The 17th, too, is a treacherous riverside hole calling for strong nerves, particularly on the approach shot, while the 18th is a par 5 that must be reckoned as a two-shot hole for the professionals, with a demanding approach to be played over a lake.

Palmer's cavalier style

Arnold Palmer's playing style was exciting to watch. He never ducked a challenge and he was not afraid of taking risks. Many holes at the K Club work on the risk-and-reward basis, and this makes for particularly fascinating golf in matchplay. Throughout the course, forward thinking and accurate execution will be rewarded with better lines to greens and shorter carries over trouble. But there are also holes requiring a little less finesse and a bit more Arnold Palmer! 'Arnold's Pick' is the name of the 4th, and this par 5 can be played cautiously as a three-shot hole, but there is a suitably aggressive option as well. Requiring a hefty carry over a bunker-strewn hill, the Palmer line is fraught with danger, but is rewarded with a shot at the well-bunkered green.

With hole after hole of lush grass, clear waters and mature trees, it is difficult to believe that the course was completed only in 1991. The fertile soils of Kildare produce the notably lush grass that has also made the county so popular for racehorse breeders. The famous Irish rain is obviously a contributory factor to this fertility, and the River Liffey and the many ponds and lakes on the course provide great fishing for the guests of the 5-star resort, and many a golfing hazard. In fact, given the perfect conditions and the rich history of the Kildare gentry who can trace their history back over 1,500 years, it is almost surprising that the K Club was not created earlier.

With tournament play of the highest calibre, bolstered by a second Palmer course in a more links style that also hosts European Tour events, it is clear that the K Club is making up for lost time.

▶ Colin Montgomerie led out the singles matches in 2006, maintaining his unbeaten record of eight straight Ryder Cup singles. The Europeans followed his example, dominating the singles and winning a third consecutive victory.

LEFT *Played as the 8th hole in the Ryder Cup, this treacherous short hole is the 17th for normal play, the River Liffey collecting many a golf ball every single day.*

CARD OF THE COURSE

Hole	Distance (yards)	Par
1	418	4
2	413	4
3	170	3
4	568	5
5	440	4
6	478	4
7	430	4
8	173	3
9	461	4
Out	3,551	35
10	584	5
11	415	4
12	182	3
13	428	4
14	213	3
15	446	4
16	570	5
17	424	4
18	537	5
In	3,799	37
Total	7,350	72

Old Head

Old Head

Old Head Golf Links, Kinsale, County Cork, Republic of Ireland

If you suffer from vertigo or are strapped for cash think twice about visiting Old Head. It stands high above the Atlantic Ocean, with sheer cliffs plunging straight down into the pounding waves, and it boasts one of the highest green fees in Europe. Nevertheless, Old Head is a course no golfer should pass up an opportunity to play.

Old Head is a historic place, recorded in a map of AD 100 by the Egyptian geographer and mathematician Ptolemy. The Eirinn clan settled there in 900 BC, giving their name to Ireland. In 1915 the British liner *Lusitania* was torpedoed just off the headland by a German submarine, with the loss of over 1,000 lives. That incident was partly responsible for the United States entering World War I.

The atmosphere is set right from the outset when you approach the club through the ruins of a 12th-century tower. You will come across the remains of 17th- and 19th-century lighthouses as you play the 7th. But that will do for history, for what bowls the visitor over is the breathtaking setting. And because there is only just room enough for 18 holes on the headland every inch of ground is used, giving no fewer than nine holes clinging to the edge of the cliffs.

Brothers John and Patrick O'Connor bought this land in 1989 and it took four years to overcome objections before construction could commence, with the course finally opening in 1997. A raft of wise heads was engaged to design the course: Ron Kirby (who had been part of the Nicklaus design team), Paddy Merrigan (a Cork-based architect), Eddie Hackett (the talented and prolific Irish architect), Joe Carr (Ireland's greatest amateur player) and Liam Higgins (professional at Waterville).

Their biggest requirement was restraint – not of budget, but of exuberance, for the wind blows hard here almost every day, so greens could not be heavily contoured and fairways needed to be generously wide. Even so, it is a rare day when a four-ball manages to get round the course without losing boxfuls of golf balls to the Atlantic.

RIGHT *The wicked 4th fairway, clinging to the clifftop as it makes its ever-narrowing way to the distant green, itself perched right on the edge above the Atlantic.*

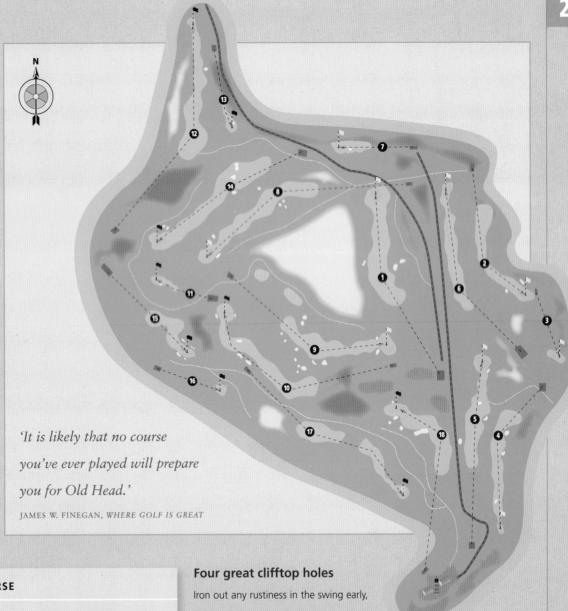

▶ Old Head was designed to be played at widely differing lengths, according to the golfer's ability. Consequently there are at least six separate teeing grounds on every hole.

▶ Kinsale has a reputation as the food capital of Ireland and hosts an international food festival each October.

'It is likely that no course you've ever played will prepare you for Old Head.'

JAMES W. FINEGAN, *WHERE GOLF IS GREAT*

CARD OF THE COURSE

Hole	Distance (yards)	Par	Hole	Distance (yards)	Par
1	446	4	10	518	5
2	406	4	11	198	3
3	178	3	12	564	5
4	427	4	13	258	3
5	430	4	14	452	4
6	495	5	15	342	4
7	192	3	16	190	3
8	549	5	17	632	5
9	475	4	18	460	4
Out	3,598	36	In	3,614	36
			Total	7,212	72

Four great clifftop holes

Iron out any rustiness in the swing early, for you will need perfect execution (and steady nerves) to survive the 4th, a dogleg played from a clifftop tee to a narrow fairway threatened by cliffs on the left all the way to a green raised up and perched directly on the cliff's edge, overlooked by the lighthouse of 1853 vintage, a constant reminder of the dangerous nature of these treacherous waters. You will be required to drive across a corner of the cliffs on the par-5 12th, and, once again, the green clings perilously to the edge of the cliffs – no place for a left-handed slicer! That is true also of the 13th, a long par 3 with yet another wonderfully sited green on high ground with the now almost obligatory drop to perdition on the left.

Finally in these world-class holes there is the 17th, another par 5, this time falling to a green set at the end of a long descent with the ocean, on this occasion, a constant threat on the right.

▶▶▶ Courses 21–29

▶▶▶ North America

Is there a greater golfing nation than the United States? The answer has to be no. It has produced more world-class golfers, and has more golf clubs and courses, than any other country, and the number and variety of its golf resorts is amazing. Through its huge buying power it could change the whole nature of golf, yet it readily embraces the traditional: Augusta National and Winged Foot are great courses and, importantly, great clubs.

In most respects Canada is similar, except that its golfing season is curtailed by the severity of its winter. However, Canada can claim to have beaten the United States to forming a properly constituted golf club, Montreal Golf Club (later Royal) having being founded in 1873.

A word of caution: unlike in most of the rest of the world, where a visitor can often turn up, pay a green fee and play almost any course, in North America many clubs are strictly private – the only visitors allowed being members' guests. However, the good news is that public-access courses are plentiful, and resort courses include some of the finest in the world.

Augusta

Augusta

Augusta National Golf Club, Georgia, USA

Tennis at Wimbledon or Flushing Meadow, motor racing at Le Mans or Indianapolis, racing at Longchamp or Churchill Downs, golf at St Andrews or . . .? Most people, even those who have little knowledge of golf, would probably answer, 'Augusta National'. Its modern-day fame comes from its hosting of the Masters, the first major of the professional golfing year, and the only major held annually on the same course. But that fame would not have arisen had it not been for one Robert Tyre Jones, or Bobby or Bob, depending on which side of the Atlantic you come from.

Jones was the greatest amateur golfer of all time, winning five US Amateur titles and one Amateur Championship in Britain. But he was also good enough to take on and beat the best professionals of the day (the 1920s) taking the US Open on four occasions and the British Open on three. Having won the Amateur and Open Championships of America and Britain in the same year, 1930, he retired from competitive golf, much to the relief of the rest of them!

BELOW *Catch your drive perfectly and you can take advantage of this downslope to reduce the playing length of the 10th hole significantly. The raised green is not one to miss.*

Jones's unlikely design partner

When Jones came to establish his ideal golf course, on which he and his wealthy friends might play, he had some novel ideas about how it might be set up, making the best players feel seriously tested while somehow allowing the high-handicapper to get round in 100 or so without feeling like abandoning golf for good. And it was a pure accident that led Jones to find the ideal architect to help him realize this concept. In 1929 Jones had been knocked out of the US Amateur Championship unexpectedly early. That year the event was held at Pebble Beach, California, so he took the

CARD OF THE COURSE

Hole	Distance (yards)	Par
1	435	4
2	575	5
3	350	4
4	205	3
5	455	4
6	180	3
7	410	4
8	570	5
9	460	4
Out	3,640	36
10	495	4
11	490	4
12	155	3
13	510	5
14	440	4
15	500	5
16	170	3
17	425	4
18	465	4
In	3,650	36
Total	7,290	72

opportunity to play nearby Cypress Point and Pasatiempo, courses designed by Alister MacKenzie, a Leeds physician turned golf course architect – one of the very best in the world in fact. Jones knew immediately that he had found the right man for the job.

Although today's course is little altered from the original (a new 16th hole and revisions to the bunkering) it is set up for the Masters in a manner far removed from what Jones or MacKenzie could have anticipated. Quite simply, the greens are maintained at frighteningly fast speeds, and trees and rough have been planted where previously there were neither. It provides a spectacle for television and it prevents scores becoming ridiculously low, but no high-handicapper would survive a hole, let alone 18!

Yet it remains a fabulous (and fabulously beautiful) course. How often we viewers are on tenterhooks as the leaders pass through the treacherous Amen Corner (11th, 12th and 13th holes) with Rae's Creek awaiting just the tiniest slip up. Will they risk all and try to get on the 13th and 15th greens in two? And there are – to us – impossible putts on the 16th and 17th greens. Or how about that slick, downhill 8-footer on the last green that must go in or we are into a play-off? The Masters is always dramatic.

▶ Augusta is ablaze with azaleas during the Masters. Before it was a golf course, this was a nursery, Fruitlands, owned by a Belgian horticulturalist, Baron Berckmans, who popularized the azalea in America.

▶ When Tiger Woods won the 2001 Masters he became the first player to hold all four majors at the same time (having won the US Open, Open Championship and USPGA the previous year). He was 65 under par for the four tournaments.

A COVETED INVITATION

The Masters is unique among the majors for having an invited field of under 100 competitors of whom a number will be amateurs. The spectators, too, are a select group, tickets being guarded jealously by those lucky enough to have them, for they are not available for public sale, and any spectator behaving in an inappropriate or unsporting manner will have their ticket confiscated in what is effectively a life ban. Consequently the same patrons return year after year, their collective experience adding to their generous support for every player, giving the Masters' galleries a deserved reputation for knowledgeable and considerate support. In this, of course, they are upholding the traditions for sportsmanship embodied by Bob Jones.

The 13th (below), 16th (main picture) and 12th (top right) are favourite holes with Masters' spectators, for each hole witnesses great drama every day: an unlikely birdie or eagle, perhaps, or an undesired skirmish with the water and a rapid tumble down the leader board.

Kiawah Island

Kiawah Island

Ocean Course, Kiawah Island Golf Resort, South Carolina, USA

Never has a name rung so true as 'The Ocean Course', for the Atlantic Ocean is in view on every single hole. Ten holes are directly on the coast, the greatest number of seaside holes on any course in the northern hemisphere, and the other eight play parallel to them. This remarkable feature not only provides some of the most scenic golf imaginable, but also makes the course massively affected by the wind. Interestingly, as with the 17th at Sawgrass, this trademark was not intended by the designer Pete Dye, who had planned to sit the course behind the dunes until his wife Alice suggested raising the course in order to provide the stunning sea views.

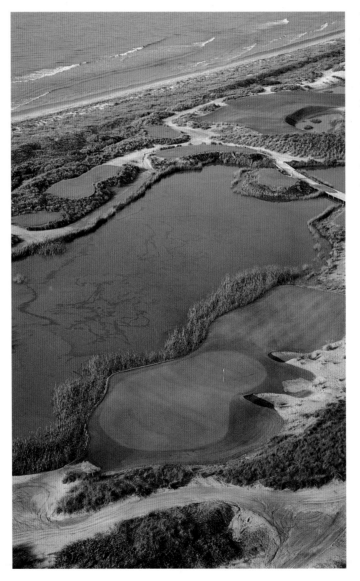

The unbelievable beauty of the course disguises its brutal difficulty. Dye made use of the natural environment, with dunes and tall grasses devouring poor shots. The most distinctive design feature is that different shot options are always available. Many holes reward daring carries, but players are never forced to take these lines. From the tee and fairway, players must pick a shot to suit their ability and the conditions.

The wide range of options makes for innovative golf, and it is also mandatory on a course so affected by the wind. It has been estimated that wind changes can alter club selection by up to eight clubs, so there needs to be a route for every strength and direction of wind.

Extensive lakes and vast tracts of sandy waste await the inaccurate shot, making this a fine matchplay course but the very devil on which to keep a medal card going.

LEFT *Like the 17th at Sawgrass, Dye wondered if the par-3 17th was dramatic enough, so he added an enormous lake to carry!*

RIGHT *The sand areas are not considered hazards so you may ground your club. This is the par-4 9th hole.*

'The biggest diabolical thing on the whole golf course.'

PETE DYE'S DESCRIPTION
OF THE 2ND HOLE

N

Creative challenges

The par-5 2nd hole is a good reflection of the course. From the tee, players will be struck by the epic view towards the ocean. But they will also be faced with golfing dilemmas in choosing the correct angle from the tee to cross the marshland that spells golfing disaster if you come up short. A safe shot plays out right for the less bold. If the drive was overly cautious, the second shot must be laid up short of another marsh, 110 yards/101 m in front of the green. Good players should be able to get around the green in two, but that is not the end of the story, as the green is a difficult raised shelf, rolling away into a deep bunker. After a gentle opening hole, the 2nd can be a real nemesis, and even the professionals rack up big scores here. In the 1991 Ryder Cup, Seve Ballesteros won the 2nd with a double-bogey to Wayne Levi's 8!

Like a true links, the options for shot-making are endless, and the longer holes tend to offer a route in on the ground, as well as an airborne approach. You are continually challenged to think hard and pick the right shot. With the design so demanding of creative golf it is no surprise that the Ryder Cup was such a success – the PGA Championship in 2012 should be a real treat.

CARD OF THE COURSE

Hole	Distance (yards)	Par	Hole	Distance (yards)	Par
1	395	4	10	439	4
2	543	5	11	562	5
3	390	4	12	466	4
4	453	4	13	404	4
5	207	3	14	194	3
6	455	4	15	421	4
7	527	5	16	579	5
8	197	3	17	221	3
9	464	4	18	439	4
Out	3,631	36	In	3,725	36
			Total	7,356	72

Oakmont

Oakmont

Oakmont Country Club, Pennsylvania, USA

Oakmont is a family course, owing its whole concept and being to Henry Fownes and his son William. Henry was an exceedingly wealthy steel magnate who purchased a large plot of land near Pittsburgh in 1903 with the idea of creating a world-class golf course. William subsequently became one of America's best amateur golfers, winning the 1910 US Amateur Championship and twice playing in the Walker Cup, and was also very influential within the political side of the game. Between them, they created something approaching a golfing behemoth, and had the clout to ensure that it was used for the most prestigious tournaments.

As first built the course was long but not particularly difficult. It was William who beefed it up in the 1920s, making it so unforgiving that it has been called the toughest course in America. For starters he set about rebunkering the course. At one time there were 220; today about 175 remain. For these Fownes devised a venomous rake; it created golf-ball-sized furrows in the sand, which were drawn across the line of play to make escape almost impossible! And then there were the greens, quite unlike any others, a remarkable assortment of sizes and shapes and, in particular, slopes. To make them the most terrifying greens in the world he had them rolled with huge barrels of sand, insisting that absolutely no watering was done to them.

The greens were also cut phenomenally low – shaved – and with the deep, clinging rough grown in to narrow the fairways for a major tournament the course fully justified its macabre reputation. Today's professionals are used to tricked-up courses with lightning-fast greens, but, with the exception perhaps of Augusta, they rarely play courses with such contours to the greens.

Great design

Surprisingly, Oakmont is not grotesque. It is handsome (more so since the removal of a great many trees that had threatened to choke the course) and strategic and responds to thoughtful play. The 3rd hole, for instance, is famed for its Church Pew bunkers – deep sandy trenches separated by rows of treacherous grass ridges – but the greater interest is provided by the green, which is difficult to access, being raised up to repel anything but the truest of approach shots. Miss this green and that's when the scrambling starts.

A glance at the card might suggest that the 17th would be a pushover for today's powerful champions. Not so! It can be driven, but that involves successfully carrying a minefield of bunkers on the left (the direct line from the tee) and somehow managing to squeeze the ball on to the putting surface between another bunker and deceptive low ground to the left. The hole can be played conservatively but it is dangerously tempting to attack and remarkably resistant to it. And that seems to sum up so much about Oakmont.

LEFT The famous Church Pew bunkers separating the 3rd and 4th fairways. As can be seen from this photograph, the bunkers to the right of the fairway are hardly less intimidating!

CARD OF THE COURSE

Hole	Distance (yards)	Par	Hole	Distance (yards)	Par
1	482	4	10	435	4
2	341	4	11	379	4
3	428	4	12	667	5
4	609	5	13	183	3
5	382	4	14	358	4
6	194	3	15	500	4
7	479	4	16	231	3
8	288	3	17	313	4
9	477	4	18	484	4
Out	3,680	35	In	3,550	35
			Total	7,230	70

▶ Describing Oakmont's one-time bunker rakes, Jimmy Demaret said, 'You could have combed North Africa with those and Rommel wouldn't have got past Casablanca.'

▶ In 1973 Johnny Miller scored an unbelievable 63 in the last round to win the US Open. It is considered by many to be the greatest round of golf ever played.

Pebble Beach

Pebble Beach Golf Links, Pebble Beach, California, USA

Pebble Beach is universally regarded as one of the world's best public courses. It was chosen as the venue for the 100th US Open in 2000, the fourth time it had hosted the US Open, yet anybody can simply book a tee time and play on this historic stage. There are, of course, two snags: it is very expensive and you must book long in advance.

Pebble Beach opened in 1919 and ten years later became the first course west of the Mississippi to host the US Amateur Championship. A young Jack Nicklaus capped an impressive amateur career here when he won the 1961 US Amateur. The 'Golden Bear' was again victorious when Pebble Beach staged its first US Open in 1972. Despite coming second to Tom Watson in 1982, his affection for Pebble Beach never waned, and eventually he bade farewell to the US Open here in 2000, an emotional Nicklaus poignantly sitting on the fence behind the 18th tee, surveying one of the best finishing holes in golf.

The par-5 18th requires nerves of steel as the entire hole teeters on the edge of the Pacific. It really should be played as a three-shot hole, often with a 3-wood from the tee. In the 2000 US Open, even the apparently infallible Tiger Woods, who would coast to victory by a margin of 15 shots, managed to pull his tee shot into the sea.

Tom Watson showed the perfect way to play the closing holes at Pebble Beach in the 1982 US Open. With one of golf's most famous chip-ins, he made birdie from the rough on the par-3 17th to claim a one-shot lead over Nicklaus. Sensibly Watson hit a 3-wood for position from the 18th tee and laid up with his second shot in the fairway with a 7-iron to leave himself a short iron approach. Again he played safely, approaching the heart of the green as the pin was tucked in behind the front bunker. From there he finished in style, rolling the 20-ft/6-m putt into the centre of the cup for a birdie, birdie finish.

Glorious coastal holes

Stunning holes are abundant here, and from the 4th there are seven consecutive oceanside holes, including the amazing 7th – with wind blowing into your face and the ocean awaiting if you overhit your shot, the prospect from the tee is nerve-racking (*see* photograph page 59). The sequence from the 8th to the 10th is one of the greatest trios of consecutive par 4s in world golf. At the 8th, after an exciting drive, you play an awesome approach shot across a corner of the ocean to find the typically small and unreceptive green.

Throughout the round you are presented with daunting drives at undulating fairways, but it is the approach shots where ingenuity is called for. On one hole with wind behind, only a high fade will stop on the tiny green, but on the next you may be playing straight into the wind and having to hit a low punch shot. With a course designed for such inventive golf, and backed by breathtaking views, many golfers would share Jack Nicklaus's view that this is possibly the best course in the world. As Billy Andrade once said, 'It's the Holy Grail for us.'

▶ In 2001 *Golf Digest* ranked Pebble Beach the No.1 course in America , the first time a public course achieved this position. It's a course that everyone wants to play, and it will cost you around $500 to do so.

▶ 17-Mile Drive, which passes through Pebble Beach, is a private toll road. The Pebble Beach Company owns the copyright on all photographic sites on this scenic route – and there are a lot of them!

LEFT *One of the best-known, and most photographed, closing holes in golf, the 18th at Pebble Beach, hugging the Pacific Ocean for every one of its 543 yards/497 m.*

CARD OF THE COURSE

Hole	Distance (yards)	Par
1	381	4
2	502	5
3	390	4
4	331	4
5	188	3
6	513	5
7	106	3
8	418	4
9	466	4
Out	3,295	36
10	446	4
11	380	4
12	202	3
13	399	4
14	573	5
15	397	4
16	403	4
17	178	3
18	543	5
In	3,521	36
Total	6,816	72

'I've loved this course from the first time I saw it. It's possibly the best in the world.'

JACK NICKLAUS

Pine Valley

Pine Valley

Pine Valley Golf Club, Clementon, New Jersey, USA

Pine Valley has a reputation for being the hardest course in the world. Yes, the Ocean Course at Kiawah Island might play considerably harder from the back tees in a gale, and many a modern layout, with water on all 18 holes, could be tricked up to be almost unplayable. But, on a daily basis, Pine Valley is the hardest simply because it asks the golfer to play total golf on every single shot, with the penalty for failure dire. What is so extraordinary about Pine Valley is that no one who has played it would begrudge it a single dropped stroke. It is a masterpiece.

It was a Pittsburgh hotelier, George Crump, a fine amateur player in his own right, who came up with the idea for this course. He had clear views about what he wanted to achieve and for some five years he lived on the site, directing construction. However, he was wise enough to consult others, including Walter Travis and Jerome Travers, two of America's leading amateur golfers in the early years of the 20th century, and the English architect Harry Colt. Quite how much each of them contributed may never be known, but Crump died in 1918 before the course was finished. Today's 12th to 15th holes were completed by Hugh Wilson, the genius of Merion, probably with advice and input from Hugh Alison, Colt's design partner.

Pine Valley today is rather different from the course that was completed in 1919, in that hundreds of thousands of trees have matured to add to the existing perils. Essentially there are tees, narrow strips of grass, which might be called fairways, swathes of sandy waste and a dense forest – and fiendish greens.

BELOW *The shortest hole at Pine Valley, the 10th, is a wicked little hole. The target is tiny, and missing it is likely to call for miraculous powers of recovery.*

▶ It used to be said that nobody could break 80 on their first visit to Pine Valley. Someone who did was a young Arnold Palmer. He won enough money from bets with the members that he was able to get married!

BELOW *The 5th hole remains extraordinarily demanding with 21st-century clubs and balls. What it must have been like with those of 1919 hardly bears thinking about.*

The ultimate in punitive golf

There are no weak holes at Pine Valley, but three in particular have world renown – the 5th, 7th and 13th. The 5th is a brutal 'short' hole – a full carry of around 230 yards/210 m over a lake and up a hill to a raised green isolated in the woodlands. It would be intimidating at half its length.

Most famous of all the holes is the 7th, a remarkable par 5 made infamous by Hell's Half Acre, a huge expanse of sand splitting the fairway between 285 yards/261 m and 385 yards/352 m from the tee. Get your drive wrong and you cannot clear it with your second. Get the drive right but mishit the second and you are still facing disaster. Get your first and second right and you are left with a devilish pitch to a green entirely surrounded by sand.

It is something similar on the 13th. You drive over a wilderness to an island fairway in the far distance. Then follows a terrifying shot, all carry, of 200 yards/183 m or more over scrub and sand to a green angled away to the left with no margin for error front, back, left or right. Yet despite the difficulties of each hole there is amazing variety to the course, with welcome change of pace, particularly within the two-shot holes. Hard yes, but still we come back for more.

CARD OF THE COURSE

Hole	Distance (yards)	Par
1	421	4
2	368	4
3	198	3
4	451	4
5	235	3
6	387	4
7	636	5
8	326	4
9	459	4
Out	3,481	35
10	161	3
11	397	4
12	337	4
13	486	4
14	220	3
15	615	5
16	475	4
17	345	4
18	483	4
In	3,519	35
Total	7,000	70

TPC Sawgrass

Stadium Course, TPC Sawgrass, Ponte Vedra Beach, Florida, USA

When the two-year-old course hosted its first tournament, the Players Championship of 1982, the professionals were almost unanimous in their verdict: they hated it! Although the design had always aimed to be tough, clearly it was too much, and Pete Dye, the renowned US golf course designer, modified the course slightly to soften the greens and change particularly brutal bunkers. The changes worked and the Players Championship has now become the unofficial fifth major.

The professionals' opinions were especially important at Sawgrass as TPC (Tournament Players Club) courses are owned by the PGA (Professional Golfers' Association) for the purpose of hosting tournaments. The course is respected by the professionals as the clever design does not favour a specific type of player. Long hitters like Davis Love and Tiger Woods have won the Players Championship, but so have those relying on accuracy such as Hal Sutton, Justin Leonard and Tom Kite. Adam Scott won at the age of 23; the following year Fred Funk won aged 48.

The island green

The PGA ownership is reflected in the design, in that the course was created for tournament golf. Huge amounts of earth were removed from the site and used to create spectator mounds surrounding the fairways and greens, the deep holes left from excavation being filled with water, creating plentiful lakes. Such is the fame of the island-green 17th, one of golf's most feared short holes, that an American sports channel devotes itself to showing uninterrupted coverage of the hole during the Players Championship. Interestingly, Dye never intended the 17th green to be surrounded by water. He was planning to make it a giant bunker until his wife suggested the island.

Water comes into play on most holes, notably on the brutal 18th. With a lake on the left of this tough dogleg, players are faced with a 'bite off as much as you can chew' concept from the tee. If the drive is not perfectly placed you must lay up the approach, as an aggressive second shot, especially from the clingy rough, tends to be water bound.

> 'We have seventeen pretty good holes at the TPC and one bad one – the 17th.'
>
> TOM KITE

▶ The weight of the Spanish tiles on the roof of the Mediterranean-style clubhouse is equivalent to two jumbo jets.

▶ It is estimated that over 100,000 balls are scooped out of the water on the 17th hole every year.

LEFT *The hole they all copy: the 18th at TPC Sawgrass, with its invitation to bite off as much as you dare with 40,000 spectators watching you.*

CARD OF THE COURSE

Hole	Distance (yards)	Par	Hole	Distance (yards)	Par
1	392	4	10	424	4
2	532	5	11	535	5
3	177	3	12	358	4
4	384	4	13	181	3
5	466	4	14	467	4
6	393	4	15	449	4
7	442	4	16	507	5
8	219	3	17	137	3
9	583	5	18	447	4
Out	3,588	36	In	3,505	36
			Total	7,093	72

You don't have to hold your breath for the course to kick in on the 17th. One of the best holes is the reachable par-5 2nd. With palm trees lining the fairway an accurate draw is required from the tee. The hole is deliberately kept at a realistic length so that it is hittable in two, but the second shot is played to one of Dye's trademark small greens, with penalizing rough and pot bunkers offering ample protection.

Recent alterations to the course have emphasized the 'hard and fast' style of the design. The result of this is that a wayward shot now has even more chance of running away into trouble, which has been increased through the addition of 200 newly planted trees. The length of the course has changed little since it was first built, only about 200 yards/183 m having been added in nearly 30 years. The emphasis, then, is on creating exciting golf through reachable distances – refreshing in an era when too many other courses are put on steroids for tour events! The biggest change is a new clubhouse in the 'stately home' style.

ABOVE AND RIGHT *The 17th hole has acquired a notoriety all of its own. On the opening day of the Players Championship in 1984 no fewer than 64 balls were hit into the water under blustery conditions. The stroke average was 3.79, making it the hardest par 3 in Tour history to that date.*

Valhalla

Valhalla

Valhalla Golf Club, Louisville, Kentucky, USA

When Tiger Woods walked purposefully towards the first tee of the 2000 US PGA Championship at Valhalla, he stopped and winked at a commanding-looking old man in the crowd, joking: 'You're awfully well dressed to be sitting out here!' The man was Dwight Gahm, founder of Valhalla. Gahm had dreamed of creating a major championship course, not to make a profit but to give something back to the game. He bought a 486-acre/197-ha plot of rolling land and commissioned golf's great champion, Jack Nicklaus, to design the course. Nicklaus described the land as 'a golf designer's dream because there is a variety of terrain, vegetation and water to work with'. After considering 40 possible routings, the course was finally completed in 1986.

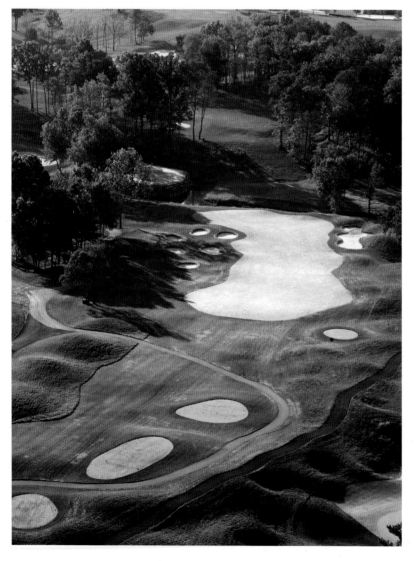

The quality of the course was instantly recognized and Valhalla was chosen to host the 1996 and 2000 PGA Championships. Valhalla is refreshingly original, made up of two very different nines. The front nine is reminiscent of a heathland course, with wide, sloping fairways confined by mounds of thick Kentucky bluegrass. The inward nine is built on higher, tree-covered terrain and plays more like a traditional parkland course. The difficulty of the course is consistent through both nines.

Heathland meets parkland

One of the more unusual holes on the course is the 7th, featuring a double fairway. The safer route is to the right, but you cannot reach the green in two. You can from the left-hand fairway but the drive is tough, with serious rough awaiting if the fairway is missed.

Summing up the challenges is the par-5 10th. The tee shot must be aimed centre right, as anything too far right will find a new fairway bunker, while anything left is blocked by trees. Even after a good drive most will lay up as the hole plays a serious 590 yards/539 m from the back. The dangers around the green include a large slope behind the hole so that long shots will run away, a tough bunker short and the thick rough that accompanies every hole. The green itself has two distinct levels and you must find the correct tier to avoid three-putting.

The signature hole is the 13th, the shortest par 4 on the course but just as testing as the long holes. Most players take an iron from the tee for safety as the landing area is riddled with bunkers. You have to be on the fairway to have a chance of finding the small green perched on a bed of rocks almost totally surrounded by water.

Valhalla is now owned by the PGA of America. The PGA has always wanted to own a number of select courses from which to run major championships, and Gahm realized that Valhalla would be guaranteed tournament golf if he sold it to them. So far it has proved a perfect venue, inspiring wonderful golf watched by thousands of spectators seated in the natural amphitheatres around the greens. As promised, Gahm chose not to make a profit out of the game; he sold the course for exactly what he had paid. His reward came with the realization of a dream – with Valhalla hosting the 2008 Ryder Cup and thereby taking a seat at the great hall of golfing mythology.

▶ In Norse mythology, Valhalla is the great hall where the souls of dead warriors feast and rejoice with the gods.

LEFT *Although Jack Nicklaus was one of the most powerful players of his era, he has always made room for the short two-shot hole in his designs. This is the 13th.*

CARD OF THE COURSE

Hole	Distance (yards)	Par
1	450	4
2	535	5
3	210	3
4	375	4
5	465	4
6	495	4
7	600	5
8	190	3
9	420	4
Out	3,740	36
10	590	5
11	210	3
12	470	4
13	350	4
14	215	3
15	440	4
16	510	4
17	475	4
18	545	5
In	3,805	36
Total	7,545	72

N

'That's as good as it gets.'

TIGER WOODS, AFTER WINNING
THE 2000 US PGA CHAMPIONSHIP
AT VALHALLA

Winged Foot

West Course, Winged Foot Golf Club, Mamaroneck, New York, USA

The winged foot is the emblem of the New York Athletic Club, a group of whose members founded the golf club of the same name in 1923. Given that Winged Foot is one of New York's premier clubs, located just off the I-95 New England Thruway, and no more than half an hour from central Manhattan, you might expect the place to be noisy, bustling and full to the brim with golfers on every hole. Nothing could be further from the truth.

For a start Winged Foot has two courses, the West, which is the championship course, and the East, which is pretty much its equal. The clubhouse is palatial, and the members know how to relax on a golf course. And yet they do not dawdle on the round. The club expects matches to take no longer than four hours, even in tournaments.

Both courses were laid out by Alfred Tillinghast, an architect of considerable lasting fame in the United States, with Baltusrol, Baltimore and Bethpage State Park sharing with Winged Foot the honour of hosting US Open Championships. The founding members wanted 'a man-sized course', and they got it. What 'Tilly' had to work with was largely flat parkland – not, you might think, the most promising canvas. But surely the sign of a great architect is to be able to produce a great course despite the lack of helpful topography, and here he produced two great courses.

RIGHT *Tillinghast's short holes are a study in themselves, so often imaginatively created from unpromising terrain. The 10th at Winged Foot West is one of his absolute best*

Tillinghast's masterly greens

'If it has not got anything about it that might make it respectable, it has got to have quality knocked into it until it can hold its head up in polite society,' was Tillinghast's philosophy, and the quality he knocked into Winged Foot was particularly on and around the greens. They are nearly all raised up above the generally flat fairways, mischievously contoured and punishingly bunkered. Fortunately Tillinghast's design blueprints survive (he worked in minute detail) and to their credit the club has been able to restore the greens to their original size and contours.

Even from the members' tees Winged Foot West is long. Unless you can drive a good distance you will find yourself banging away with wooden-club approaches and if you are not devilishly straight you must surely tangle with the defensive bunkers or lack the control necessary to get the ball close to the pin on these tough greens. And when there is a shorter par 4, such as the 6th, the entrance to the green is incredibly narrow, with the putting surface seriously canted and hidden behind a right-hand protective bunker.

There are moments of respite on the short holes, but, again, only if you can find a way past the narrow entrances and guardian bunkers. Each of the greens is raised sufficiently to reject the shot that is not quite good enough. One of those short holes, the 10th, is world class, played across a valley to a plateau green loyally attended by punitive bunkers. A bewildering putting surface awaits if you do make it safely on to the green. Such is the genius of Tillinghast, whose courses should be on every golfer's wishlist!

▶ During the 2006 US Open the 1st and 18th were the joint most difficult holes against par, both averaging 4.471. The only hole to have an average score below par was the par-5 5th, which averaged 4.654.

▶ Winged Foot may look natural to the eye, but it was actually created by blasting 7,200 tons of rock and felling 7,800 trees. It took a workforce of 200, with 60 teams of horses and 19 tractors, to complete the task.

CARD OF THE COURSE

Hole	Distance (yards)	Par
1	450	4
2	453	4
3	216	3
4	469	4
5	515	5
6	321	4
7	162	3
8	475	4
9	514	4
Out	3,575	35
10	188	3
11	396	4
12	640	5
13	214	3
14	458	4
15	416	4
16	478	4
17	449	4
18	450	4
In	3,689	35
Total	7,264	70

Banff Springs

Stanley Thompson 18, Fairmont Banff Springs Hotel, Banff, Alberta, Canada

Early golf courses simply evolved. Golfers found a route through whatever natural obstacles they found where they had chosen to play. There was minimal earth moving. The emergence of the earliest course architects, such as Old Tom Morris, towards the end of the 19th century was accompanied by earth moving on a very small scale – as much as a couple of men with shovels or possibly with a horse and scraper could move. Enter the steam shovel. It could hardly move mountains, but it could shift a large amount of dirt in a day. Throw in dynamite and almost anything became possible, or it did if you had a huge budget.

The enormous Banff Springs Hotel belonged to the Canadian Pacific Railway (CPR). It was the jewel in their crown, standing proudly overlooking the Spray and Bow Rivers surrounded by the stunning scenery of the Rocky Mountains. It had had a golf course of sorts since 1911 but it hardly matched up to the rest of the facilities on offer at this world-class hotel. The CPR had money and they also had railway trucks, trainloads of them. They had seen what Canadian architect Stanley Thompson had achieved at their rival railway Canadian National's resort at Jasper Park, so they hired Thompson themselves.

LUCKY ACCIDENT

Banff's most famous hole, the 4th, Devil's Cauldron, was not part of Thompson's original plan. He had no intention of using this area of the extensive property. However, during the winter of 1927, when heavy snows and bitter temperatures had halted construction work, an avalanche created a new glacial lake. When Thompson returned to Banff he spotted the lake and its potential as the basis for a world-class short hole immediately.

The world's most expensive golf course

It took Thompson and his team two years to build the Banff course, and when it opened in 1929 it was said to be the most expensive course ever built. The great thing about the course is that you would never guess that Thompson had spent so much money and moved so many thousands of tons of earth, for it all looks so natural. And what the unsuspecting eye might not notice is that a lot of Thompson's creativity went into ensuring that manufactured features, such as bunkers, raised greens and mounds, were perfectly scaled to the grandeur of the surrounding forests and mountains. As a result of such empathy, the course is not overwhelmed by the scenery.

In recent years a new clubhouse has been erected and the original order of playing the holes abandoned. So the course now starts with a hole that throws the golfer straight into the forests. The next two holes turn to face Mount Rundle. Thompson needed dynamite to blast away enough room to build the 3rd fairway. Further dynamite was required to clear the site for the 4th green, but it was well worth it, for the 4th is a world-class short hole (so good that *Golf Magazine* ranks it in the top four in the world), calling for a drop-shot down over a glacial lake to find a well-bunkered green on the far side. After three more holes in the forests the course emerges for a sequence of beautiful holes alongside the Bow River.

Thompson's original opening hole is now the 15th and many an experienced golfer has stood on that tee and been knocked off their game by the sight ahead, with the sparkling Spray River far below and the tree-lined and bunker-strewn fairway uncomfortably distant on its far side.

▶ Because it is too remote from major centres of population Banff Springs has never hosted an important professional tournament.

▶ Banff Springs is in the middle of a vast national park. Deer are frequently found on the course and bears are occasional visitors.

LEFT AND BELOW
Wonderful golf in an exquisite setting. Stanley Thompson's course at Banff Springs is exceptional – the 4th hole is, quite simply, one of the greatest holes in golf.

CARD OF THE COURSE

Hole	Distance (yards)	Par
1	415	4
2	180	3
3	535	5
4	200	3
5	430	4
6	380	4
7	610	5
8	160	3
9	510	5
Out	3,420	36
10	225	3
11	425	4
12	450	4
13	230	3
14	445	4
15	480	4
16	420	4
17	385	4
18	585	5
In	3,645	35
Total	7,065	71

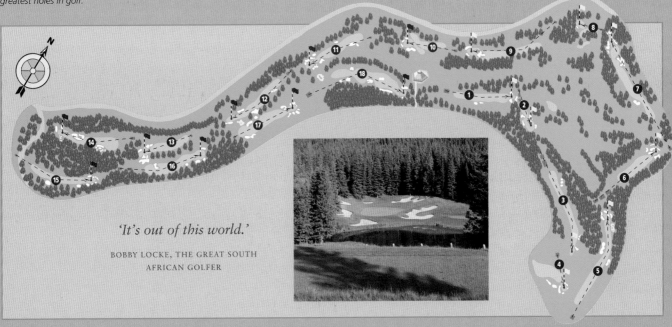

'It's out of this world.'

BOBBY LOCKE, THE GREAT SOUTH
AFRICAN GOLFER

▶▶▶ Courses 30–33

Caribbean, Central & South America

Golf first came to South America towards the end of the 19th century when British engineers travelled to Argentina and Brazil to build railways and set up factories. As in many other parts of the world the British (and the Scots in particular) were the evangelists for the game. Early courses were established close to the major centres of population and, inevitably, they were somewhat exclusive. Climate, geography, political unrest and demography have been factors in keeping down the growth of golf since then, although the achievements of Roberto de Vicenzo and Angel Cabrera emphasize that there is no shortage of talent.

Engineering techniques learned in the Far East during World War II and the Vietnam War were put to use to enable golf courses to be built in the hot and steamy jungles close to the Equator. The development of grass strains capable of providing viable putting surfaces has made it possible to create golf courses of an international standard in Central America and the Caribbean. With the expansion of Mexico's tourist industry has come a raft of high-class, big-name resort courses.

Casa de Campo

Casa de Campo

Teeth of the Dog Course, Casa de Campo Golf Club, La Romana, Dominican Republic

Golf grew up by the sea: first in Scotland, later in England and Ireland. It was inevitable that as golf spread throughout the world many of the game's finest courses were constructed along the shores of the great oceans and seas. Those early British courses played *near* the sea. Many of their successors play *over* it, few more compellingly so than the Teeth of the Dog Course at Casa de Campo.

The name of the course refers to the native coral – *dientes del perro* – which was crushed and used to build peninsula tees out into the Caribbean and for the low retaining walls preventing the precious land from returning to the sea – until the passing of an occasional hurricane, that is. It was not the only innovative practice employed in the construction of the course, the fairways and greens being neither seeded nor turfed, but planted by hand with individual tufts of grass. But then, this was never going to be an ordinary course.

It was one of the early courses of Pete Dye, arguably the most inventive of those course designers working in the last quarter of the 20th century. He had already displayed vision and creativity far beyond his thus-far limited experience at Harbour Town in South Carolina. At La Romana he was given a blank canvas, and he took himself up in a helicopter to explore every inch of this huge resort until he found a stretch of promising coastline. He delivered more than his wealthy patron could have hoped for, unquestionably the Caribbean's finest golfing challenge. Dye has been back twice more to create two further imaginative courses at this extraordinary resort, which is more a way of life than somewhere to spend a holiday.

RIGHT *The 5th is the first of Teeth of the Dog's compulsory carries over the sea. It may not be long, but the penalty for inaccuracy is obvious!*

Entrancing ocean holes

It would be wrong to ignore the inland holes, for they are testing enough, two of the first four holes being modelled on famous originals at Prestwick and Pinehurst and a third being a tribute to Charles Blair Macdonald, one of the most influential of all golden-age American golf designers. The first skirmish with the sea is made at the short 5th, an all-or-nothing par 3 from a promontory tee to a green set out into the sea. There are similar short holes at the 7th and 16th and yet in no way is there a sense of blind repetition of a good idea. Dye was too individual a character to resort to that.

Spectacular though these holes are, and lasting though they are in the mind, it is probably the two-shot holes beginning with a drive over the water that are the stars of the show. The 8th is just such an example, where you are asked to bite off as much as you can chew from the tee, but very likely tempted to try just too much. There are mirror-images at the 15th and 17th, too, part of a stirring back nine. All three courses are fascinating, but it is Teeth of the Dog that captures the heart of the golfer as well as the soul of La Romana.

RIGHT *With the sea on your left on the way out, your right coming in, play straight or give up! This is the 16th.*

▶ The newest of the Pete Dye courses, the Dye Fore Course, measures an astonishing 7,770 yards/7,105 m from the back tees.

▶ Even the fairway soil on the Teeth of the Dog Course is unconventional, being a blend of sand, dirt and a by-product of sugar refining, *cachaza*.

CARD OF THE COURSE		
Hole	Distance (yards)	Par
1	401	4
2	378	4
3	545	5
4	327	4
5	155	3
6	449	4
7	225	3
8	417	4
9	505	5
Out	3,402	36
10	377	4
11	540	5
12	445	4
13	175	3
14	505	5
15	384	4
16	185	3
17	435	4
18	440	4
In	3,486	36
Total	6,888	72

'Pete Dye discovered a natural violence at Casa de Campo well suited to his creative expression.'

ANDRE-JEAN LAFAURIE,
GOLF WRITER

Casa de Campo

BACK TO COLUMBUS

The Dominican Republic has a long European history, dating back to December 1492 when Christopher Columbus first landed on the island. It can claim the first cathedral and university in the Americas. At the Casa de Campo resort in 1976 it was decided to try to build a replica medieval European village using the techniques of the day – Altos de Chavón. It is now an artists' paradise with studios, a design school and archaeological museum with a wealthy cultural foundation to support it all. There is even a copy of a Greek open-air theatre. For golfers the best place to view all this is from the Dye Fore Course, which roams inland from the resort, overlooking the artists' village and much else, for this is a long course – 7,770 yards/7,105 m from the back tees.

RIGHT *It all looks so simple on the 7th hole when the sun is up on a calm day. The island of Hispaniola on which the course is located provides a buffer between the Atlantic Ocean and the Caribbean Sea. When the wind gets up Teeth of the Dog is a tough course.*

Cabo del Sol

Ocean Course, Cabo del Sol Golf Club, Baja California, Mexico

Baja California, with its enviable climate (350 days of sun per year), was bound to catch on as a holiday resort at some point. As far as the Mexicans were concerned it might as well have been another country, for apart from a tiny strip of continuous land at the very north of the peninsula it is separated from the mainland by the many hundreds of miles of the Sea of Cortes.

The Americans and Canadians solved its accessibility problems by flying in, which they now do in considerable numbers, in the early days to fish or whale-watch. It was inevitable that they would want to play golf, too, and the two contrasting courses at Cabo del Sol provided a very potent seed from which further developments are arising.

To confirm to the travelling public that Cabo del Sol is a top-of-the-range resort, two of the great names of golf course design were commissioned to lay out courses – Jack Nicklaus and Tom Weiskopf. Nicklaus was unquestionably the greatest golfer of his era (many would say of all time) and a master player at demolishing a golf course, but his own-design courses are more generous to the average

player than you might expect. He took to heart the adverse criticisms of his early designs, 'too hard and made for Nicklaus'. Weiskopf, on the other hand, had one of the most elegant swings of all time and a formidable technique, yet did not achieve as many major results as were once forecast. His golf courses, however, are frequently far more thought-provoking than those of some of the more prolific winners among his contemporaries.

BELOW *The 17th hole, played across the beach even from the very front tees, is beautifully routed to align with the distant peaks.*

CARD OF THE COURSE

Hole	Distance (yards)	Par
1	436	4
2	574	5
3	327	4
4	555	5
5	458	4
6	190	3
7	207	3
8	438	4
9	469	4
Out	3,654	36
10	436	4
11	352	4
12	515	5
13	213	3
14	366	4
15	530	5
16	429	4
17	178	3
18	430	4
In	3,449	36
Total	7,103	72

▶ Although golf tourism is relatively new to this part of Mexico, tourists of another kind colonized the area in the 1730s: the Spanish, who established a presidio in San José del Cabo. Nor are modern tourists only golfers – fishing is big here, too.

ABOVE RIGHT *The 13th, the only inland par 3 on the Ocean Course, is a fine hole, played downhill to a green defended by bunkers, cacti and scrub.*

Desert and ocean

Cabo boasts two completely different styles of course. Weiskopf's Desert Course was built inland, a rugged course (admittedly with fine ocean views) that asks the golfer contemporary questions of length, accuracy and finesse. Nicklaus's Ocean Course is in many ways gentler, although there are compulsory carries over the Pacific on the 5th and 7th, 17th and 18th holes. Yet, to the competent player, water carries are hardly intimidating. What the good player might enjoy more is the challenge of the approach shots to the 5th and 16th, whose greens are deceptively set up on the very edge of the ocean and therefore call into question the golfer's trust in the yardage and commitment to the shot. Psychological golf can be such fun!

The Jockey Club

The Jockey Club

The Jockey Club, San Isidro, Buenos Aires, Argentina

At the 2007 US Open, the world found out that Argentinian golf is seriously underrated as Angel Cabrera stormed to victory; the same goes for Argentinian golf courses. Few would consider this country for a golfing break, but the region is home to some fine courses, the best being the Jockey Club.

Founded in 1882 for the polo-playing social elite, the club decided to add golf to its activities in the 1920s. Wisely, they hired Alister MacKenzie (who already had Royal Melbourne and Cyprus Point in his portfolio) to design two courses on an area of land they had purchased. MacKenzie accepted, pleased to escape from the depression engulfing the United States where he was then living, but he soon found himself staring at a grimly flat landscape. His solution was to create the signature features of both courses: the countless artificial mounds that adorn both fairways and greens. MacKenzie adored St Andrews and he recaptured much of its spirit on

this very dissimilar terrain. It is often said that golf course architects should be judged by their work on unpromising land. MacKenzie robustly proves that contention here.

The Blue Course is the shorter of the two, and accuracy is called for to navigate its tight fairways. In a final salute to St Andrews, the 9th and 18th greens are joined together to create a stunning double green, divided by one of the many substantial mounds. Though both courses are similar, it is the longer Red Course that has seen tournament action, including the 2001 Argentine Open, won by none other than Angel Cabrera.

RIGHT *The extraordinary mounds surrounding the 16th green are closely shaven to give multiple options for a recovery shot.*

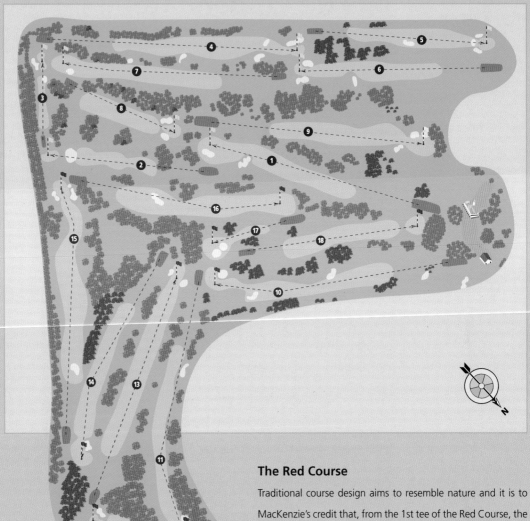

▶ In 2005 Kevin Stadler won the Argentine Open (in its centenary year) at the Jockey Club to become the only father/son winners in the tournament's history – his father, Craig, having triumphed in 1992.

CARD OF THE COURSE

Hole	Distance (yards)	Par	Hole	Distance (yards)	Par
1	425	4	10	470	4
2	350	4	11	506	5
3	148	3	12	175	3
4	490	5	13	444	4
5	340	4	14	390	4
6	355	4	15	511	5
7	425	4	16	401	4
8	208	3	17	170	3
9	415	4	18	354	4
Out	3,156	35	In	3,421	36
			Total	6,577	71

The Red Course

Traditional course design aims to resemble nature and it is to MacKenzie's credit that, from the 1st tee of the Red Course, the mounds sweeping the fairway look entirely natural. It is also apparent that these mounds are a major strategic feature, many easily as tall as a golfer, and there will rarely be a flat lie or straight fairway roll. That is not to say that the course is needlessly penalizing. MacKenzie designed courses to be enjoyable to play, and this becomes evident on the 2nd. At just 350 yards/320 m, this is far from the slog of too much modern design, but the hole must be played with skill as the green is mountainous. Creativity is called for, with the design urging players to dream up running shots and long-range putts in true links spirit. The undulations provide such a thorough test that it was even debated whether the course needed bunkers at all.

Today the Jockey Club represents something of an oasis. When you walk down the bunkerless 18th, backed by the thumping of thoroughbred hooves from the adjacent polo field and racecourse, it is hard not to be smitten with the traditional atmosphere. This charming course has something different to offer to the more distance-orientated modern game. Argentina truly is an underrated golfing destination.

Ilha de Comandatuba

Ilha de Comandatuba

Comandatuba Ocean Course, Ilha de Comandatuba, Una, Bahia, Brazil

Brazil's reputation is more one of stunning beaches than of stunning golf courses, but the Hotel Transamérica Ilha de Comandatuba resort shows the two need not be independent of each other. Cut off from the mainland by a river, the resort is considered an island, and 13 miles/21 km of private beach skirt the hotel. Sitting between the sea and the mangrove swamp is an eye-catching golf course, the creation of American architect Dan Blankenship, who has crafted the unusual character of the land he was given to work with into a highly original design.

The Ocean Course plays five of its holes along the sea, features 12 lakes on nine of the holes, and incorporates the retreating beach in the style of a desert. Vast expanses of sand surround the fairways, eliminating the need for rough, and as the sand is so compacted it is eminently playable – a far more appealing prospect than endless rough, given that the majority of golfers here are holidaymakers. Nature, in the form of coconut trees and forest vegetation, provides a perfect backdrop to the lush fairway grass and contrasting sand dunes, and from this tropical foliage emerge countless exotic birds, capuchin monkeys, foxes and anteaters to add to the unique environment of the course. The use of Bermuda grass for fairways and a dwarf Bermuda for greens helps present the course well, despite the climate.

Multiple choice

Given the extraordinary location, the hole design is suitably idiosyncratic, as fairways balloon around lakes and sand, giving the golfer several options on each shot. Scoring well requires golfers to be decisive in judging the correct line for their skill. On the par-5 12th, you are even confronted with parallel fairways (though they eventually merge into one). Short hitters are advised to drive down the right-hand fairway, but they risk running out of room from the more forward tees. Big hitters may be tempted to try for the left-hand fairway, leaving a better approach shot, but a mighty carry is required over the sand that surrounds the entire hole and cuts in front of the green.

Another par 5, the 5th, offers a choice of ways to drown! At some point most golfers are going to be tempted to shorten the route to the green – probably with dire results. The whole golfing experience is hugely enjoyable, with the monstrous 18th, played along the coastline, offering a picturesque finale to the round – though those prone to slicing could easily end up on the beach, racing towards the water.

▶ The hotel built Brazil's biggest private airport to cater to its guests who, in addition to the golf and luxury spa, can take surfing and circus lessons and go deep-sea fishing for giant blue marlin on Charlotte Bank.

RIGHT *An aerial view of Isla Comandatuba reveals just how much sand has been incorporated into the course.*

LEFT *Somewhere out there is a fairway – reaching it from the back tee calls for a sure technique and steady nerve.*

CARD OF THE COURSE		
Hole	Distance (yards)	Par
1	412	4
2	192	3
3	408	4
4	367	4
5	596	5
6	162	3
7	397	3
8	432	4
9	511	5
Out	3,477	36
10	379	4
11	416	4
12	518	5
13	217	3
14	399	4
15	480	4
16	293	4
17	187	3
18	562	5
In	3,451	36
Total	6,928	72

▶▶▶ Courses 34–41

▶▶▶ Continental Europe

Golf was introduced to many European countries by the British: to France in 1856 at Pau by retired soldiers, to Belgium in 1888 at Antwerp by English businessmen, and to Portugal in 1890 near Oporto by members of the port wine trade. As golf spread, clubs were formed where there were international communities, near the major cities and in and around the fashionable spas.

In the early years of the 20th century two British course designers, Tom Simpson and Harry Colt, were particularly active in Europe, but golf was an elite pastime and few courses were required. That was not the case in Germany where golf enjoyed huge popularity before World War II, and a fine native designer, Bernhard von Limburger, emerged.

All changed with the coming of the jet aeroplane, cheap holidays and the birth of golf tourism. Demand for resort golf in countries such as Portugal and Spain spawned a new generation of international and home-bred course designers as Europe's potential was tapped, while the fall of Communism in Eastern Europe has opened up a burgeoning golf industry there.

Le Golf National

L'Albatros Course, Le Golf National, Guyancourt, France

Built on flat land, nowhere near the sea, and with 353,000 cubic yards/270,000 cubic metres of artificial lakes, it may seem preposterous to liken Le Golf National to a Scottish links. But when the wind gusts over the dunes, through the ashen rough and straight into your face, the similarities become clear. In true links fashion, the course is open to the elements, but the design also features the lakes and stadium golf of an American TPC course. It is this mix of styles that creates the course's main defence, as one is called upon to be creative, playing links shots as well as target golf.

Popular French golf only really took off in the 1970s when the economic potential of the game was realized. Courses sprang up all over the place, spearheaded by a new wave of course architects. The effects of this golfing revolution are apparent today, with a sudden influx of good French professionals. Le Golf National is probably the most important course to come out of this era, becoming the permanent home to the French Open Championship.

The course must have seemed somewhat of a gamble when it was proposed. Not only was the country new to the golfing buzz, but the land was also far too flat to fulfil the brief: to create France's first course capable of hosting regular tournaments. Two years later, after the transportation of 400 trucks of earth a day, the course was both undulating and teeming with bunkers and lakes, and plentiful spectator mounds.

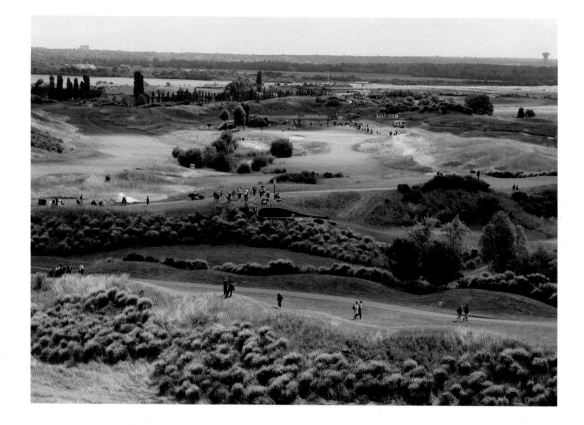

RIGHT *In many respects this bleak, windswept site resembles a links, but what it cannot have is true links turf and genuine seaside sand dunes.*

▶ There is a shorter 18-hole course, L'Aigle, which has a distinctly Scottish feel to it, and a charming nine-hole course for training.

BELOW *The short 16th is one of several holes on the back nine with treacherous water carries.*

'*All the shots you have to play offer multiple choices.*'

SEVE BALLESTEROS

CARD OF THE COURSE

Hole	Distance (yards)	Par	Hole	Distance (yards)	Par
1	415	4	10	377	4
2	202	3	11	191	3
3	530	5	12	437	4
4	439	4	13	410	4
5	404	4	14	552	5
6	377	4	15	421	4
7	443	4	16	175	3
8	207	3	17	470	4
9	563	5	18	514	5
Out	3,580	36	In	3,547	36
			Total	7,127	72

Scotland meets Florida

All these features are apparent from the 1st tee. The fairway is narrowed by a large lake on the left, which also adds intimidation to the approach shot. Bunkers mark the right-hand edge of the fairway before the land turns to dunes. At 415 yards/379 m, position is more important than length, and a 3-wood down the right-hand side gives the best line at the enormously long green. From here there is great diversity in holes, but one must take early birdie chances, as the course gets consistently harder.

Looking down the fairway from the 15th tee, you really could be in Florida, with an expansive lake on the right dwarfing the playing surface. Inevitably most shots are played too cautiously down the left, but this leaves a long approach to a green almost surrounded by the vast lake. In the 1991 French Open, seven balls were lost in the lake by a three-ball!

On the opposite side of the lake, the 18th is almost a mirror image of the 15th. Water stretches all the way down the left side of this par 5. But the fairway is wide and, with a relatively easy approach over the water, it is possible to finish in style. Unlike Retief Goosen, who was five shots clear on the tee in 1997 and opted to lay up short of the water. He topped the ball into the water and finished with a seven to win by only three!

Sporting Club Berlin

Sporting Club Berlin

Faldo Course, Sporting Club Berlin, Bad Sarrow, Germany

Before World War II, Germany could boast more golf courses than any other country in continental Europe. After the war the country was divided and the eastern part, the DDR, became aligned with Soviet Russia. Golf and Communism were not compatible and a number of fine old courses were abandoned, never to be restored. As an island city, surrounded by Communist territory, Berlin could not expand. It boasted a single 18-hole course and there was no possibility of room being found for any other course within the western-controlled sectors.

The fall of Communism and the symbolic dismantling of the Berlin Wall provided a stimulus for the rapid development of new courses within easy striking range of the city on former DDR territory. Given that agricultural practices in the DDR were antiquated and that much farm work was still carried out using horses it seems a pity that no developer thought to exploit those skills while they remained available in order to create a traditional course such as Colt or Simpson might have built. The results are so much subtler. Instead, developers have seen this as an opportunity to aim for the high-end market, and top of that list is the impressive resort at Bad Sarrow, Sporting Club Berlin.

RIGHT *A view of the par-5 10th hole on the Faldo Course at Bad Saarow. Faldo has a great affinity with links golf. It shows here.*

> The back nine of the Palmer-designed Champions Course runs into the woods and has been described as the most beautiful back nine in Germany.

ABOVE *Escape from the bunkers on the Faldo Course needs strength, skill, commitment and nerve. These are on the 17th.*

Big name designers

You can add millions of dollars to the construction bill for a new course if you persuade a famous golfer to put his name to the design. For that money you might get two or three single-day visits from the great man, the design work being carried out by the full-time architects in his team. Nick Faldo is something of an exception, taking a rather greater personal interest in the detailed design of 'his' courses than most. His links-like course at Bad Sarrow has already attracted much favourable comment. It makes a fine contrast with the Arnold Palmer woodland course at the same resort. There is a third 18-hole course by Stan Eby, plus exemplary practice facilities.

The Faldo Course was intended to hold professional tournaments right from the start (it has hosted a number of German Opens), but Faldo was not to be tempted to make this course a long slog. Interestingly, he has included a number of shorter par 4s in the repertoire, and water – the seemingly obligatory element of any new design with championship aspirations – is blissfully absent, being a factor only on the par-5 1st and 10th holes. It could hardly be a links course without bunkers and Faldo has seen to it that there are 133 of them, most of the deep pot-bunker variety.

Flat the land may be, but there are abundant features to the course, with angled greens such as at the 7th, narrow entrances to them such as at the 9th, and always the thought that if you finish in the wrong part of one of these bunkers you are almost bound to lose a stroke.

> SC Berlin is not just about golf. It is one of Europe's finest sports resorts, offering tennis, riding, sailing on the largest lake in Brandenburg and excellent spa facilities.

CARD OF THE COURSE

Hole	Distance (yards)	Par	Hole	Distance (yards)	Par
1	548	5	10	559	5
2	414	4	11	570	5
3	186	3	12	376	4
4	379	4	13	233	3
5	213	3	14	415	4
6	533	5	15	391	4
7	439	4	16	360	4
8	382	4	17	193	3
9	447	4	18	458	4
Out	3,541	36	In	3,555	36
			Total	7,096	72

Kennemer

Kennemer

Kennemer Golf & Country Club, Zandvoort, Netherlands

It would be all too easy to assume that the Netherlands is entirely flat. True, much of it is, but there would be no Netherlands at all without a chain of sand dunes along its North Sea coast preventing the briny waves from invading the bulb fields and meadows on which much of the nation's wealth was founded. Three excellent courses are to be found in these dunes: The Hague, Noordwijk and Kennemer.

In many ways Kennemer is rather like Royal Lytham and St Annes on England's Lancashire coast. Both are actually a short distance inland from the sea, behind popular seaside resorts (Zandvoort and Blackpool), and both have the company of a railway line for a few holes. There the resemblance ends, for Kennemer's dunes are wilder and more imposing than Lytham's. Nevertheless, there is something of a British feel to Kennemer due, in part, to the thatch-roofed clubhouse but, more fundamentally, to the fact that the course was designed by Englishman Harry Colt, who also designed Sunningdale and Wentworth.

WARTIME DEFENCES

It's something of a miracle that Colt's course survives, because during World War II Kennemer was a concrete jungle of anti-tank walls and anti-aircraft guns, part of a big defence area surrounding Amsterdam. Astonishingly, though, the course was not totally destroyed and it was brought back into use as early as 1947. Key to this was the survival of the detailed correspondence between Colt and the club during construction.

Tumbling dunes and plateau greens

Holland's sand dunes are important not only sea-defensively but also ecologically, and there is a great feeling of being at one with nature when playing a round at Kennemer. Perhaps this is felt most while waiting on the 1st tee, a platform high on the dunes next to the clubhouse, with a rolling fairway far below making its way through dunes and scrub on either side to a distant green. This feeling continues on the 2nd, a short hole over wild country to a pinnacle green. One of the great vistas awaits on the 3rd tee, the fairway swinging left past bunkers and a tree-clad hillock en route to the green. Tracking back along the perimeter of the course on flatter ground, the next five holes, somewhat different in character, offer good scoring opportunities before the handsome 9th returns play to the heart of the dunes.

An exhilarating drive over a tumbling valley opens the back nine, and the pitch to a secretive green keeps up the fun. There is no shortage of length over the 11th and 12th holes, taking play to the far end once more. Pine trees give this part of the course more of a heathland feel, continuing through the 13th and 14th holes. Then comes the most individual hole of the lot, an extraordinary short hole played to a plateau green on top of a steep hill. There are no marks for being short, with the ball tumbling all the way down to the bottom of the hill! Three solid holes complete the round.

LEFT The 14th green and beyond it the unforgettable short 15th, precariously perched on its hilltop with bunkers far below. In the background is Kennemer's attractive thatched clubhouse.

CARD OF THE COURSE

Hole	Distance (yards)	Par
1	452	4
2	165	3
3	524	5
4	330	4
5	346	4
6	476	5
7	371	4
8	187	3
9	425	4
Out	3,276	36
10	361	4
11	460	4
12	546	5
13	373	4
14	385	4
15	163	3
16	480	5
17	168	3
18	398	4
In	3,334	36
Total	6,610	72

▶ A 17th-century painting of a young golfer hanging in the clubhouse at Kennemer is a reminder that golf in the Netherlands may well be as ancient as it is in Scotland.

▶ When the Dutch Open is played here a composite course is used, incorporating holes from the newer nine-hole Van Hengel Course, designed by Frank Pennink.

San Lorenzo

San Lorenzo Golf Course, Almancil, Algarve, Portugal

The Algarve is one of the most popular golfing destinations in Europe. It has the climate to be wonderfully attractive to Northern European golfers during the dark and cold winter months, yet Atlantic breezes help to prevent it from being unbearably hot during the summer. Golf courses litter the region – the choice is immense. But there is another side to it. The Algarve is now a maze of concrete, high-rise apartment blocks. To enjoy golf in the Algarve it is necessary to be very selective, and the course that has that little bit of edge over the others is San Lorenzo.

San Lorenzo dates from the late 1980s, a design by the American architect Joe Lee. What Lee had in his favour was a site that descends to the Atlantic Ocean and he made full use of the advantage he was given. There is another plus, it must be said. Like all other Algarve courses, San Lorenzo is woven between real-estate developments. The developments here, however, are of Hollywood-style villas and mansions adorned with Moorish ornaments. They may resemble a film set, but they are far superior to the dreaded high-rise monstrosities elsewhere.

Nature's backdrop

It is not quite true to say that San Lorenzo descends to the Atlantic Ocean. More correctly, it descends to the banks of the estuary of the Ria Formosa, which is separated from the ocean by a low ridge of sand dunes. The shelter these dunes afford to the estuary ensures a safe haven for a wide range of species of swimming, diving and wading birds. Happily, the whole area is designated a nature reserve.

While ornithologists may rush to the 6th and 7th holes, so do golfers, for it is at this point that San Lorenzo comes into its own. Both holes enjoy elevated teeing grounds from which drives are made on to narrow strips of fairway bordering the waters. There are no marks for playing too safe – the chances of finding the ball on the tree-clad hills on the left are no better than 50:50. Both greens lie perilously close to the beach, that on the 7th, unusually, bunkered behind.

For the average golfer, the 8th is about keeping out of trouble and using any handicap shots available – it is, after all, Stroke 3. But for the big hitter it is an exciting hole, with water all the way down the right and hillocks encroaching from the left where you would rather they did not.

The back nine opens with a demanding drive over an arm of a lagoon to a rising, curving fairway, but from here on – until the 17th – the round is solid rather than spectacular, handicap golfers inventing their own problems. At the 17th, however, the prospect of a watery grave looms, or else dropping a shot by playing too safely away from the lagoon. The green is threatened by water. So is the 18th green, but this time there is no safe route for the timid. At some point at least one stretch of water must be taken on and conquered.

LEFT *San Lorenzo's final green, surrounded by water and sand, is a difficult target whatever the length of the approach shot – a touch of Florida in the Algarve.*

CARD OF THE COURSE

Hole	Distance (yards)	Par
1	540	5
2	177	3
3	365	4
4	372	4
5	143	3
6	422	4
7	377	4
8	574	5
9	400	4
Out	3,370	36
10	568	5
11	383	4
12	432	4
13	393	4
14	172	3
15	517	5
16	208	3
17	376	4
18	406	4
In	3,455	36
Total	6,825	72

▶ San Lorenzo has never sought to attract professional tournament golf, and has been spared the unnatural lengthening so often imposed on Tour courses.

▶ San Lorenzo is located within the Quinta do Lago estate, although it is not part of the Quinta do Lago portfolio that includes the four Quinta courses and two Vale de Lobo courses.

San Lorenzo

PORTUGUESE RESORT GOLF

Portugal's rise in prominence from being an almost golfless country to that of being a major player in resort golf is quite remarkable. Suffice it to say that there were only three courses on mainland Portugal at the end of World War II. There are now over 50 courses and the number is rising steadily, even alarmingly. Yet this is almost entirely a business for tourists, and given the winter climate of northern Europe one understands why it should be so. In comparison with the number of golf courses there are few native players. The sad thing about this is that golf courses are developed in an 'international' style for 'international' golfers.

A comparison can be made with Vinho Verde, a Portuguese wine of no greatness, but the perfect accompaniment to *bacalhau*, that great Portuguese salt-cod dish. Have the real thing served to you in a jug and it is frothing, bone dry and utterly thirst-quenching. Drink the stuff made for tourists and it is semi-sweet, a little cloying and bottled with a fancy label. It loses its character and its honesty. Portuguese resort courses need a little more distinctive character and rather fewer fancy labels.

RIGHT *The 6th green is found only after a perfect drive from an elevated tee to a low fairway bounded by a treacherous, scrub-clad hill and the Ria Formosa.*

ABOVE RIGHT *Unusual bunkering is a feature of the 7th green, its purpose, as much as anything, to deceive the eye into thinking the target is smaller.*

Vilamoura

Vilamoura

Old Course, Vilamoura, Quarteira, Algarve, Portugal

It was Henry Cotton who first showed the world what golfing potential was on offer in the Algarve. His 1966 course in a former rice plantation at Penina, near Lagos, can be said to have started the explosion that has led to several dozen courses being constructed on the coastal strip between Lagos and Faro. Three years after Penina was completed, the pioneering course built by Frank Pennink among the umbrella pines and cork oaks at Vilamoura was unveiled. The resort of Vilamoura has grown out of all recognition since those days, but, happily, Pennink's gem remains largely unaltered: a beacon for those with eyes of something of a sleeper compared with some of the more brazen offerings being blatantly promoted today.

Pennink was a British architect of Dutch background, a fine amateur player, a connoisseur of all that is best in golf and, incidentally, a gifted and stylish writer on all matters golfing. From the start, Vilamoura oozed class. It was not in Pennink's armoury to resort to 'eye-candy' – he was too honest for that. In fact Pennink's laid-back style was all about subtlety, which is why it is all the more pleasing that nobody has ever been brought in to 'tart the course up'.

Trees, trees, trees

Vilamoura's fairways have become narrower over the years. The umbrella pines that line each fairway are undoubtedly attractive, but they are also constrictive, their spread increasing with each year's growth. Straight hitting is clearly essential to good scoring. With pines as the principal defence Pennink had little need for fairway bunkers, and throughout the round it is Pennink's restraint that shines through. The course received a major overhaul in 1996, under the sensitive guidance of Martin Hawtree, with the overall conditioning being greatly improved.

The Old Course starts gently, with a short par 4, a par 5 reachable in two shots, and another short par 4. Then comes the only water hazard on the course (what a contrast to so many of the neighbouring courses!), a duck pond on the par-3 4th. It will trouble only a really terrible shot, the more pertinent obstacle being a tree on the direct line to the green. The par 3s are among the best holes on the course. Following this, the par-5 5th returns us to the clubhouse, a hole with fewer trees and consequently more prolific bunkering. Greater length of tee shot is required over the next three holes, and strong hitters will certainly fancy a crack at driving the 9th green, but its defences are strong – Pennink was a wily golfer.

In the opinion of many, the 12th is the finest hole of the round, an admirable dogleg requiring perfect shot placement for success, and with no need for more than minimal bunkering. And a single fairway bunker is all that is required to turn the par-5 16th into a model exercise in control. Bring your brains to the Old Course. Take your brawn to its neighbours. Class will out!

LEFT *Pennink's honesty is shown in this aerial view of Vilamoura. He simply made the most of what he was given – natural undulations and umbrella pines.*

BELOW *The problems of excessive tree growth on an artificially watered course are plain to see in this view of the 11th hole.*

▶ So prolific are the courses in this part of the Algarve that the Old Course is one of seven owned by Oceânico. Their new Faldo Course is described as having an Arizona desert style!

CARD OF THE COURSE

Hole	Distance (yards)	Par
1	339	4
2	476	5
3	354	4
4	178	3
5	531	5
6	232	3
7	430	4
8	458	4
9	290	4
Out	3,288	36
10	167	3
11	427	4
12	533	5
13	381	4
14	481	5
15	164	3
16	562	5
17	386	4
18	452	4
In	3,553	37
Total	6,841	73

El Saler

Parador de El Saler, Valencia, Spain

Some 10 miles/16 km south of Valencia is a stretch of rippling sand dunes and pine forests on a narrow strip of land between the expansive wetlands of the Albufera National Park and the unspoilt beaches of this part of Spain's Mediterranean coast. In the 1960s, before golf tourism had taken off in Spain, it was decided to add a golf course to the facilities on offer at the luxury hotel, the Parador Luis Vives. Javier Arana, a gifted Spanish architect largely unknown outside his native country at that time, was called in to design the course. El Saler, his finest creation, remains, after his death, a magnificent testament to his talent.

Although there are a number of links-like holes in the dunes closest to the sea, El Saler is for the most part a pine-forest course with generous, undulating fairways and expansive greens. Arana's bunkers are in scale with the course, seriously proportioned, although their flat floors make escape relatively simple – that is until you perish in one of the deep bunkers in the dunes, very possibly through the back of the green when escape is made to a green running downhill, away from the shot, testing even for the best.

Golf at one with nature

An abundance of wildlife, particularly many species of birds of the forest and wetland, is found at El Saler, and a post-golf tour of the Albufera is heartily recommended. Such abundant flora and fauna suggest a healthy environment. In parallel, the course is maintained in a cultured condition, although the price to pay for this is slow greens – if they were kept fast-running they would disappear under the scorching, penetrating sun in no time at all.

Starting off amidst the pines, the first four holes introduce us to most of the trademarks of Arana's style, with fairways characterized by deceptive ridges that make distance judgement and tee-shot placement subtly challenging – you have to think your way round here, not simply blast away unimpeded. Suddenly, on the 5th, the whole feel of the course changes with a tee shot uphill towards a distant ridge. And on the far side there is a most attractive panorama, with the fairway rushing downhill towards a green constructed in the dunes, and a wide seascape beyond.

From here to the turn this links-like atmosphere is maintained, with the sweeping, up- and downhill par-4 6th, one of the best holes on the course, and a monster dune on the 8th. These holes set El Saler apart from so many other Spanish pine-forest courses. That said, the 10th is a handsome way to return to the pines, with a characteristically sited green, raised up amidst the pines and ingeniously bunkered.

After a somewhat pedestrian passage, the course revisits the dunes for a stunning finish, with the 17th green enfolded in sandy hills and treacherous chasms. From the final tee there is a marvellous seascape to the right, although a golfer's mind should be on the matter in front, for this is a difficult, sloping, curving fairway to hit and there is serious trouble in the dunes to the right. For good measure the green is typically tricky, with many slopes to contend with should you fail to find the right part of it.

▶ El Saler has staged few professional tournaments, but these have included the Spanish Open, Turespaña Masters and Seve Trophy. Bernhard Langer scored a remarkable 62 when winning the 1984 Spanish Open. His fellow competitors were so astonished that they suggested that he had left out two holes.

LEFT *There is no denying the links challenge of the drive at the last hole, with its distant, sloping fairway and all manner of sandy perils to the right.*

CARD OF THE COURSE

Hole	Distance (yards)	Par
1	428	4
2	376	4
3	532	5
4	189	3
5	515	5
6	442	4
7	358	4
8	359	4
9	156	3
Out	3,355	36
10	399	4
11	568	5
12	198	3
13	348	4
14	414	4
15	564	5
16	428	4
17	213	3
18	466	4
In	3,598	36
Total	6,953	72

Valderrama

Valderrama

Club de Golfe Valderrama, San Roque, Cadiz, Spain

Regarded by many as the top golf course in continental Europe, Valderrama is inextricably linked with the Volvo Masters, the European Tour's end-of-season flagship event. In 1997 it hosted one of the most closely fought Ryder Cups, with Seve Ballesteros's European team managing to withstand the comeback of the Americans on the final day to retain the Cup by a margin of one point. Despite its high profile, and the menacing reputation of the 17th, Valderrama prides itself on being playable by all skill levels. A large range of tees ensures not only widely differing yardages, but also different routings, to cater to various abilities. Credit must go to the inventive design of the course, which, interestingly, was designed twice by the same man.

Valderrama began its life as the New Course at Sotogrande, in turn becoming Las Aves, before being bought by rich Bolivian industrialist, Jaime Ortiz-Patiño. Keen to host high-quality tournament golf, Ortiz-Patiño called back the designer of the course – the prolific architect Robert Trent Jones – to make alterations. Most significant of these changes was to reverse the two nines so the hardest run of holes would become the finishing stretch. A massive drainage programme was initiated and, later, a lake was introduced in front of the 17th green. Conditioning is always impeccable.

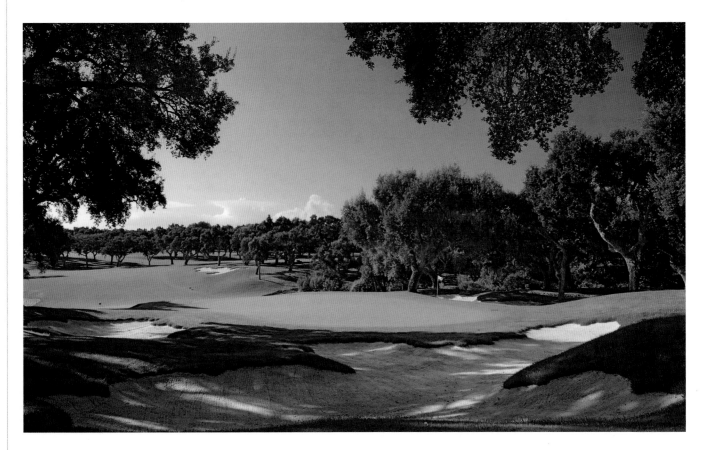

Shades of Augusta

Overall length has never been a priority at Valderrama but the challenges are considerable. The course is hilly, wind is a constant factor – and a variable one, with two prevailing winds changing the characteristics of the course from day to day – and a proliferation of trees makes particularly high demands on straight hitting. The trees remove options from play. Usually there is only one specific route to the green, meaning that this is target golf.

One of Ortiz-Patiño's aims was to replicate the feel of Augusta, both in condition and design, and this is achieved well on the 10th. Despite its short length, there is little room for error as the tee shot must be faded past a lake on the right and short of a bunker that devours a tee shot hit too straight. From here one has a magnificent view of the green, surrounded by white sand bunkers and a ring of cork trees. But, like the 9th at Augusta, the approach must be hit positively, as a weak shot will roll backwards off the green and often back down the fairway!

The environment plays an important role in the Valderrama experience, and the natural beauty of the course is a shining example to others. An active involvement in ecology means that there are twice as many species of plant and a third as many more types of bird on the course than in the surrounding countryside. While many courses resort to fertilizer, pesticide and even dyeing the lakes blue, Valderrama has maintained quality without neglecting the environment. In fact, US Ryder Cup captain Tom Kite claimed the greens to be among the best he had ever putted on.

▷ Huge sums are spent each year on maintaining the course in peak condition. Valderrama has 4,600 sprinklers, compared to the 600 for the average course in the United States.

LEFT *This view of the short par-4 10th shows why yardages are irrelevant, even at professional level, if the topography of the site and the intuition of the architect are in harmony.*

CARD OF THE COURSE

Hole	Distance (yards)	Par
1	389	4
2	399	4
3	173	3
4	535	5
5	381	4
6	163	3
7	461	4
8	345	4
9	441	4
Out	3,287	35
10	364	4
11	547	5
12	197	3
13	402	4
14	370	4
15	200	3
16	422	4
17	511	5
18	434	4
In	3,447	36
Total	6,734	71

'Awesome.'

FRED COUPLES, ON HIS FIRST
GLIMPSE OF VALDERRAMA

NOTORIOUS 17TH

At 511 yards/467 m, the par-5 17th at
Valderrama ought to be a picnic to the
professionals, but this is actually one
of the most controversial holes in golf.
Like many of the holes on this course,
it begins with a challenging drive to
a bunker-adorned fairway lined by
cork trees. After a slight dogleg right,
the front of the green is guarded by a
lake, with a steep mound behind the
putting surface housing three bunkers.
The controversy arises because the
green slopes dangerously towards
the water, as Tiger Woods found out
with a triple bogey in the 1999 World
Golf Championship. At the 1997
Ryder Cup, the 17th was criticized as
the green was deemed unfair. Colin
Montgomerie famously described it
as 'the worst hole in Europe', perhaps
not the most tactful thing to say
considering the hole was redesigned by
the European captain, Seve Ballesteros!
But the hole showed its undeniable
strength: to create drama. It was an
instant favourite with the emotional
fans who swarmed on the bank behind
the bunkers to witness the few who
proved it could even be reached in two
and managed to hold the green.

RIGHT *In the heat of the Ryder Cup or the*
pressure of other professional tournaments
the 17th is a nervous moment for the players.
It can make spectacular viewing for the gallery.
But is it great architecture when seemingly
perfectly played shots to the green are
inconsistently rewarded?

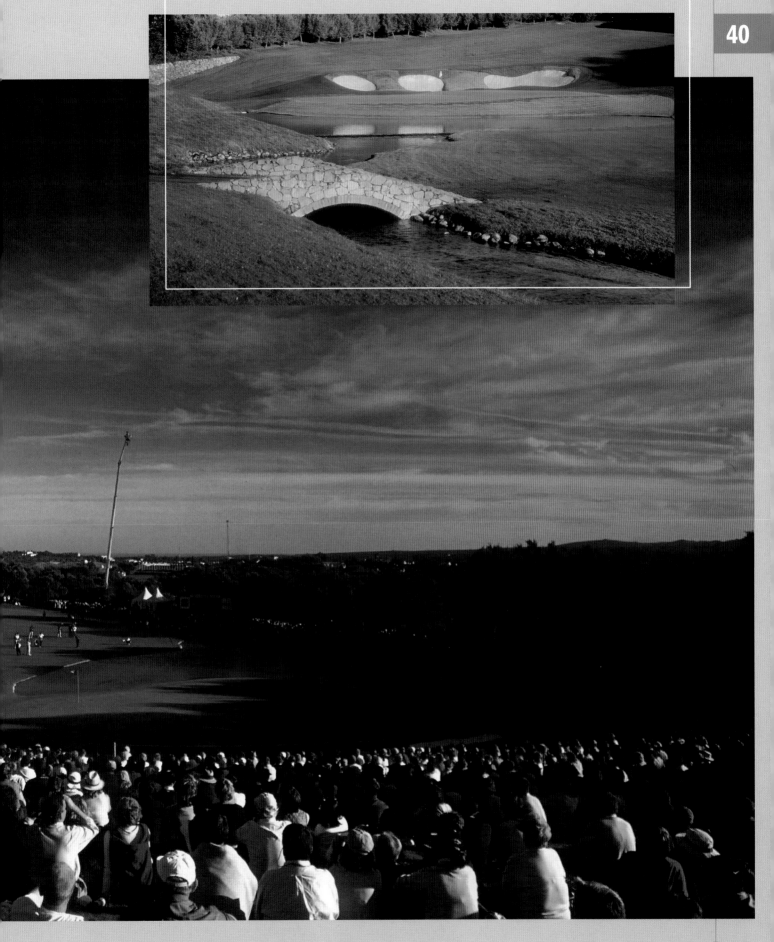

Crans-sur-Sierre

Golf Club Crans-sur-Sierre, Valais, Switzerland

The European Masters and, before it, the Swiss Open have attracted quality fields to Crans-sur-Sierre every year since 1948, plus the one prewar Swiss Open held at Crans in 1939. It has produced some famous winners: Garcia, Donald, Els, Romero, Westwood, Montgomerie, Ballesteros, Olazábal, Stadler, Faldo, Woosnam, Price, Locke, Rees, Nagle and Charles to name but a few. They enjoy playing here: they like the place; they like the atmosphere; they like the winner's cheque; they like the golf course. After all, it usually produces very low scoring.

The first course at Crans was set up in 1905, opening the following year with a nine-hole layout, which was expanded a few years later to 18. It did not survive World War I. A second attempt at establishing a course, again of nine holes, was made in 1921. That was superseded by an 18-hole course that opened in 1929. It was designed by an Englishman, Harry Nicholson, and remained largely intact until 1997 when Seve Ballesteros was commissioned to rebuild the greens, add a little difficulty around the course, and create some new back tees.

LOW SCORING

It was at Crans-sur-Sierre in 1971 that the Italian golfer, Baldovino Dassù, recorded a 60, the first time anyone had achieved it on the European Tour. Against the par of the day this worked out at an astonishing 13 under par. Colin Montgomerie holds the 72-hole scoring record for Crans at 260. He closed with rounds of 61 and 63 to win by four shots.

RIGHT *The 7th is one of the easiest holes on the course, a drive-and-pitch hole of only 331 yards/303 m, but who could not be exhilarated by such a spectacle!*

Stunning scenery

If you were to set down the Crans course in the middle of flat farmland it would attract little attention. It is perfectly good but nothing remarkable in itself. What sets it apart – very much apart – is the ravishing scenery. It is not every day that you get to pitch to a skyline green backed by a towering, snowy Alpine peak. Against such massive backdrops the golf course can seem minuscule. In fact it is far from minuscule, measuring a healthy 6,937 yards/6,343 m from the white tees, with a par 5 stretching to 629 yards/575 m and the longest par 4 being 503 yards/460 m. That said, the course sits at an altitude of some 5,000 feet/1,500 m which enables longer hitting.

The course opens with a reachable par 5 before doubling back for a sturdy two-shot hole, followed by a short hole along the course boundary. In the past, the 4th was played as a par 5, but now it is a super-long par 4, and even from the visitors' tees it measures a healthy 487 yards/445 m. Length is less significant on the dogleg 5th, pine-enclosed 6th, wide-open 7th and well-bunkered 8th but then comes the extraordinary 9th, wending its way relentlessly to its green near the clubhouse.

On the back nine there is another sharply doglegged hole, the 12th, and back-to-back par 5s. You and I play the 16th as a short par 4, but for the European Masters it is shortened to a 235-yard/215-m par 3, bringing the overall par down to 71. Two straightforward par 4s then bring us home.

▶ There is a second, nine-hole, course at Crans, designed by Jack Nicklaus. It is hoped eventually to extend this course to 18 holes.

▶ Crans is possibly the best example of a place where the course map, or course statistics, tell little of the golfing experience.

CARD OF THE COURSE

Hole	Distance (yards)	Par	Hole	Distance (yards)	Par
1	540	5	10	405	4
2	439	4	11	205	3
3	191	3	12	410	4
4	503	4	13	200	3
5	339	4	14	595	5
6	324	4	15	516	5
7	331	4	16	346	4
8	175	3	17	386	4
9	629	5	18	403	4
Out	3,471	36	In	3,466	36
			Total	6,937	72

▶▶▶ Courses 42–44

▶▶▶ Middle East & Africa

Resort golf may be new to the Middle East and Africa but golf has been played there for many years. The great problem for all but the southern part of Africa was climate. Grass would not grow at all in the arid climates of North Africa and the Middle East. Grass would grow in the hot and wet equatorial lands, but it was impossible to grow fine grasses. Golfers had to improvise.

The easy bit was simply to carry a carpeting mat around with you. You could stick a tee peg in it for the drive and treat yourself to a perfect lie for subsequent shots. Greens were a greater problem and the solution found was to have sand greens, rolled flat and then oiled so that the surface did not blow away. It provided a remarkably true putting surface and was easily repaired. Such greens are still in use here and there and were common in the southern states of the United States until scientists developed grass strains capable of producing an acceptable surface even in fierce heat.

In the Middle East the water required to grow the grass is more expensive than oil!

Emirates

Emirates

Majlis Course, Emirates Golf Club, Dubai, United Arab Emirates

The Emirates Golf Club was dubbed 'The Desert Miracle' when, in 1988, it became the first grass course in the Middle East, and it is easy to see why. Sheikh Mohammed bin Rashid Al Maktoum, of the Dubai ruling family, donated the property and urged that the course should reflect the natural state of the land. Karl Litten's design was an instant success, creating lush Bermuda-grass fairways of a kind more usually associated with Augusta National, while protecting them with the natural desert dunes.

Not only has the course succeeded in bringing grass to the desert, there are also abundant water hazards. Desalinated water is transported to the course from a nearby factory at huge engineering expense. It is achievement enough that any golf course has been constructed in such an inhospitable environment, but the fact that the course is a fine one almost makes it deserving of the accolade of a 'miracle'!

Instant recognition

The quality of the course was instantly appreciated when the European Tour chose the Majlis for the Dubai Desert Classic just one year after its completion. As a result the course can already boast a considerable history for one so relatively young. Drama is often created around the excellent 18th, a long par 5, which doglegs around a lake. A simple lay-up is sensible, but the temptation is to cut the corner and risk finding water. Then the approach shot is also over a stretch of water that has claimed the errant shots of many a great player. Both Ian Woosnam and Tiger Woods have lost the championship from near-certain victory by finding water with approaches at 18. But it is a rewarding hole if played well, perfectly demonstrated by Ernie Els, who struck a majestic 6-iron to 22 feet/7 m and rolled the putt in for eagle to claim victory by one shot in 2005.

▶ Ernie Els holds the course record 61, which helped him to victory in the 1994 Dubai Desert Classic. He also won the tournament in 2002 and 2005.

▶ Tiger Woods won the 2008 Dubai Desert Classic in stunning fashion, taking just 31 strokes on the back nine to catch and overtake Els in the final round.

LEFT *Linking the lush green of the fairways and greens of the Majlis Course with the barren desert beyond, the remarkable clubhouse is styled after Bedouin tents.*

CARD OF THE COURSE

Hole	Distance (yards)	Par	Hole	Distance (yards)	Par
1	458	4	10	549	5
2	351	4	11	169	3
3	530	5	12	467	4
4	188	3	13	550	5
5	436	4	14	434	4
6	485	4	15	180	3
7	184	3	16	425	4
8	434	4	17	359	4
9	463	4	18	547	5
Out	3,529	35	In	3,680	37
			Total	7,209	72

Like the 18th, many holes require a strong nerve and a great deal of accuracy to play over the picturesque oasis-like lakes, but the best-looking hole on the course is the stunning 8th. The fairway doglegs around the desert on this difficult par 4, creating a captivating view from the tee, as lush green fairway is contrasted with desert scrub. Equally impressive is the approach shot, played to a raised green backed by the dramatic clubhouse.

The clubhouse is an extraordinary sight, built in white concrete and glass; it resembles a Bedouin tented village, providing a unique backdrop for a beautiful course. Hospitality is a matter of pride at the club, and this extends beyond the superbly equipped clubhouse. Golfers are looked after out on the course as well, even provided with air-conditioned refreshment huts – it is in the desert, after all, and temperatures range from 86–122°F/30–50°C!

In 2006 the second 18-hole course, the Wadi, was redesigned by Nick Faldo. This course is also appealing, incorporating the 'wadi' (Arabic for 'valley') into the design, which, along with Faldo's trademark fairway bunkering, creates an interesting course requiring disciplined course management.

Karen

Karen

Karen Country Club, Nairobi, Kenya

Whatever the rights and wrongs of the colonization of Africa, there is one lasting legacy of former times that is more apparent in Kenya than in other such countries – a golf infrastructure. Kenya's geography and climate suit the growing of tea and coffee, and many of the golf clubs were founded in the early years of the 20th century by estate owners and farmers. Golf courses were not confined to any specific region. They were to be found all over the country.

First came the Nairobi Golf Club, started as a nine-hole course in 1906. It was given the Royal prefix by King George V and is now an expansive 18-hole course. Upcountry courses soon followed, with Nyeri leading the way in 1910. The Indian Ocean coast was also a promising golfing region and the Mombasa Golf Club dates back to 1911. Not far behind was the primitive Kisii course (1914) in the Western Rift Valley/Lake Victoria region, although the pick of the club names in that part is surely the enticing Nandi Bears Club, formed by tea farmers in 1928. Happily, the golf tourism industry in Kenya flourishes and visitors are treated to some enchanting golf in wonderful locations.

Literary origins

The essence of Kenya in those years before World War II is captured in the novel *Out of Africa* by Baroness Karen von Blixen. It was on part of her former coffee estate, in the area now known as Karen, that one of Kenya's top courses was begun in the 1930s. Karen Country Club was the product of hard work by a young banker, Remi Martin (nothing to do with the Cognac house), who was in charge of acquiring the land for the course, setting up the company to build it and developing the real estate, which was to be particularly attractive to investors because the golf course would have grass greens – as opposed to 'browns' – at that time largely

BELOW *At an altitude of 5,400 feet/1,646 m, conditions for golf at Karen are not as overpoweringly hot as might be imagined. Here golfers putt on the 12th green.*

unknown in Kenya. Such investment has paid off with a course that is maintained in fine condition, good enough to host annually the Kenyan Open on the European Challenge Tour.

Karen's golf course is as pretty as a picture, its flourishing wildlife (both flora and fauna) encouraged by an active policy of nature and wetlands conservation and promotion. Everywhere there is colour and beauty. There is also considerable variety in the nature of the golfing challenges.

The course retains the layout it has had for many years, and still plays to more or less the same length it did over 30 years ago. It has not needed to be lengthened inordinately to withstand the onslaught of today's young professionals. All that has been done is to drop par from 72 to 71, with one of the members' par 5s (the 3rd) being played as a tournament par 4. A surviving par 5 is the 2nd, a demanding hole that turns through almost a right-angle at the length of a decent drive.

▶ In the early years of the club, natural hazards included cobras (one interrupted the official opening of the club in 1937), baboons, zebra and elands — and above all lions.

CARD OF THE COURSE

Hole	Distance (yards)	Par
1	350	4
2	580	5
3	538	4
4	387	4
5	203	3
6	489	4
7	185	3
8	384	4
9	443	4
Out	3,559	35
10	362	4
11	395	4
12	301	4
13	457	4
14	137	3
15	561	5
16	195	3
17	458	4
18	559	5
In	3,425	36
Total	6,984	71

RIGHT *A fire destroyed the clubhouse in 1977 and almost caused the club to be closed. Its replacement was built in the style of a game park lodge.*

Fancourt

The Links at Fancourt, Fancourt Hotel and Country Club Estate, George, South Africa

Late on 23 November 2003, the Links played host to one of golf's greatest duels. The US and International teams of the President's Cup, tied at the end of four days of golf, sent one player each to settle the match with a head-to-head, sudden death play-off. An estimated 800 million people worldwide watched Ernie Els and Tiger Woods battle for the cup as darkness fell on the picturesque course.

With the first two holes halved, both players faced long par-saving putts on the third play-off hole. Tiger holed out from 15 feet/4.5 m to leave Els with a putt of 8 feet/2.5 m to keep the match alive. Opposing captain Jack Nicklaus later said, 'There wasn't anybody in the world who wanted to see you miss that putt,' and Els duly rose above the pressure and holed out. Captains Nicklaus and Player epitomized the spirit of the game by agreeing to a tie and sharing the cup.

Designed by Gary Player, this strikingly beautiful course sweeps through mounds at the feet of the Outeniqua Mountains, the dunes creating a links-like experience.

These mounds are often assumed to be natural because they seem so in keeping with the surrounding mountains, but they are actually the result of a huge amount of earth moving. In fact, from the mounds down the right of the 13th, there is a good view of the flat farmland that is the land's more natural state. But natural or not, the course plays like a links, those carefully created mounds enveloping the fairways and fierce pot bunkers protecting tough greens.

BELOW *The clubhouse at Fancourt reflects the atmosphere of the Manor House, the hub of the resort, where fine dining is the order of the day.*

Risk and reward

Player's trademark design features – risk and reward and playability to all skill levels – exist throughout the course. Powerful hitters have opportunities to make long carries on most holes, and there is temptation to drive both short par 4s, the 6th and 14th. However, the drives must be perfect as the holes are cleverly designed, with large pot bunkers and thick rough on the dunes ready to gobble up wild shots.

Multiple tees successfully keep the course interesting to all golfers, so an exciting contest will arise between a long hitter and a short accurate player. On all too many other courses the holes are consistently too tight for the long hitter, or too long for the player relying on accuracy. It is this element of the design that made the course perfect for the matchplay of the President's Cup, as one player could lay up safely in the fairway, allowing his partner to take on the aggressive lines.

The long par-4 15th is reminiscent of the 18th at Sawgrass, doglegging left around marshland. However, the unsung hero is the par-3 17th. With a stone-walled burn short and left, most golfers play out to the right, leaving themselves a tough chip across a slick green. Trees behind the green add confusion about wind direction. This is when you should turn for advice to one of the caddies at Fancourt, said to be among the best in the world.

FANCOURT'S FOUR COURSES

The Links is the highest profile of four courses at Fancourt. The Montagu has recently been upgraded by David McClay Kidd, designer of Bandon Dunes in Oregon, USA, while the Outeniqua is a 7,000-yard/6,400-m Gary Player design. To play these courses you must stay at the resort. The public-access course is Bramble Hill, designed by Player to give 'golfers of every level a Fancourt experience'.

CARD OF THE COURSE

Hole	Distance (yards)	Par
1	396	4
2	236	3
3	469	4
4	494	4
5	549	5
6	341	4
7	476	4
8	202	3
9	609	5
Out	3,772	36
10	408	4
11	161	3
12	481	4
13	533	5
14	361	4
15	477	4
16	584	5
17	186	3
18	616	5
In	3,807	37
Total	7,579	73

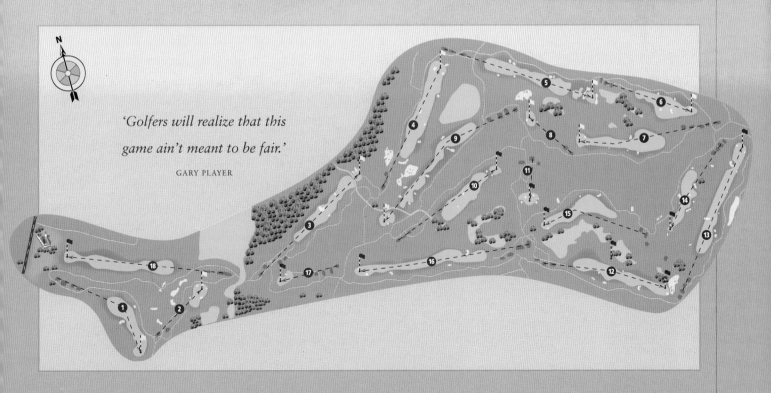

'Golfers will realize that this game ain't meant to be fair.'
GARY PLAYER

Fancourt

GETTING IT RIGHT

In order to get the links feel just right, Player (rumoured to be the world's most travelled athlete) revisited a number of links courses in Scotland and Ireland. Writing about Fancourt, he said, 'It has been designed to make golfers feel as though they were at Ballybunion, Dornoch or St Andrews, with rolling fairways, pot bunkers, big greens, high rough and a seascape appearance.'

ABOVE *The 17th, viewed here from left of the tee, is reckoned to be one of the toughest par 3s on all four courses. The humps and bumps designed to give the course an authentic links appearance are clearly visible in the background.*

RIGHT *Key to producing a links-like playing experience is scaling the artificial undulations so that they are not overwhelmed by the mountain background, aptly demonstrated here on the 12th hole.*

▶▶▶ Courses 45–50

▶▶▶ Asia & Australasia

Golf in Asia is booming. Its players, men and women, are among the most competitive and successful on the US and European Tours. Golf tourism is growing at unprecedented rates, and new courses are being built in quantity. At last China has taken hold of the sport and, with political support, golf is simply exploding there, with Mission Hills building no fewer than 12 courses: St Andrews is only halfway there after six centuries! But golf is hardly new to Asia, Royal Calcutta being the oldest club in the world outside the British Isles. On the whole, golf was played where European countries had colonies or around the great trading posts. Japan, in particular, took up golf at a high level, in the inter-war years.

Australia and New Zealand, with their traditional links to Britain, have been well stocked with good courses, many of them truly world-class. As in Asia, new course building is proceeding apace, and the quality of design is so high that any of 20 modern courses might have been included in this book, and there are many mature courses that can give them a run for their money.

Royal Calcutta

Royal Calcutta Golf Club, Kolkata, India

The Royal Calcutta Golf Club is the oldest in the world outside Great Britain, founded as the Dum Dum Golf Club in 1829. It was some 12 years before another Indian golf club was established, this time in Mumbai, and between them the two clubs fostered the game in the subcontinent. Indeed, Royal Calcutta (it became Royal at the time of the visit of King George V and Queen Mary to India in 1911) was so influential that it had a status similar to the R&A in that it was the custodian of the rules and etiquette of the game in India. The club also set up the Amateur Championship for India.

Under British rule, Royal Calcutta excluded Indian members. Happily that is no longer the case, although the club still retains its strong links with the R&A and also with a number of British clubs with which it shares reciprocal courtesy of the course. Less happily, however, the club could not afford to retain all of its former 36-hole grounds, selling off that portion further from the clubhouse to the Bengal government. What remains, however, is a formidable 18-hole test.

Unseen dangers

At first sight, Royal Calcutta appears to be benign, with flat fairways and few bunkers. What the eye has not seen is a whole network of ponds and pools and interconnecting ditches criss-crossing the course below the level of the fairway. They were created when earth was dug out to form the greens and tees and, as they are now used to store water, are known as tanks. Their positions cannot be predicted and there may be several forced carries over them on any hole.

One of the hardest holes on the course is the 7th, a solid par 4 running along the course boundary, driving out of a chute of trees towards a fairway curving to the left past water, before another tank cuts the fairway off abruptly. With the length of the drive limited, the second shot is substantial. Another strong hole on the way out is the 3rd, curving this time to the right, with a serious carry over a tank to find the fairway.

Royal Calcutta is a long course, but this is largely because, like the Old Course at St Andrews, there are only two short

RIGHT *The splendid clubhouse, which has been the spiritual home of Indian golf since 1829. It still carries with it a sense of grandeur and formality.*

holes. The par 5s are not particularly long by today's standards, but there are enough longer par 4s to keep mid- and long-irons in work. A good example is the 10th, which, yet again, involves a second shot that must carry water in front of the pear-shaped green. And so it goes on, tank after tank, until suddenly, on the last hole, there is water-free fairway. Surely there must be one more hidden tank lurking to catch the incautious somewhere before the green! But no, a single fairway bunker and a couple of greenside ones are all that remain to trap the unwary.

▶ The Cashmere Cup, presented by Royal Calcutta Golf Club to the R&A in 1882, became the trophy for the world's first handicap tournament, now known as the Calcutta Cup.

RIGHT Sheep sheltering from the heat of the sun in a bunker at Royal Calcutta. Sheep sheltering from the wind in Scotland created many of the very first bunkers.

CARD OF THE COURSE

Hole	Distance (yards)	Par
1	359	4
2	141	3
3	436	4
4	525	5
5	426	4
6	422	4
7	415	4
8	413	4
9	398	4
Out	3,535	36
10	432	4
11	410	4
12	369	4
13	194	3
14	409	4
15	502	5
16	362	4
17	371	4
18	430	4
In	3,479	36
Total	7,014	72

Mission Hills

Olazábal Course, Mission Hills Golf Club, Shenzhen, China

With 216 holes of golf stretched over 12 courses, each one carrying the name of a great golfer, Mission Hills is already established as the largest golf resort in the world. The names – or most of them – trip off the tongue: Annika, Duval, Els, Faldo, Leadbetter, Nicklaus, Norman, Olazábal, Ozaki, Pete Dye, Vijay and Zhang Lian Wei. The Nicklaus Course hosted the World Cup of 1995, the first time a Chinese course had been accredited by the US PGA. The tournament returned in 2007, but this time it was to be the first of 12 World Cups to be staged annually at the resort.

It is astonishing to see the way in which China has embraced golf. Whether charging in, building courses and resorts at an alarming rate, will be good for Chinese golf is yet to be seen, but its enormous tourism potential must be obvious to all. Mission Hills has the desirable asset of being a mere 20 minutes from Hong Kong, and the transport links necessary to get the numbers of visitors required to make a resort on this scale viable are excellent. Another great asset is the climate, which is good for golf all year round, as players in Hong Kong have known since golf arrived in 1889.

Long and heavily bunkered

For the 2007 World Cup the Olazábal Course was selected as the host. Olazábal has never been the longest (or most accurate) driver on tour, although he is an exceptionally gifted iron player. So it is something of a surprise to find that the course that bears his name is the longest of all 12 courses at Mission Hills. On this occasion it produced Scottish winners (for the first time since the tournament began as the Canada Cup in 1953) in Colin Montgomerie and Marc Warren, who had finished second in the previous year.

The long 6th, with its narrow fairway in the driving area, is probably the toughest of the par 4s. Like so many holes here the jungle background is impressive. There is a chance to enjoy this from the elevated tees of the 8th, a long and difficult par 3, and the 9th, a very heavily bunkered par 5. Olazábal is an impressive bunker player and this is reflected in the number of bunkers on the course – around 150. A large number of them appear on the 10th, the great majority of those littering the left side of the short but uphill par 4.

These days it is almost obligatory to provide a so-called signature hole. On the Olazábal Course this is the 15th. It is an all-out skirmish with the water that runs down the left of the fairway, giving the brave (or stupid) several options for cutting the corner to turn a regular par 5 into a death-defying two-shotter. This style of hole is becoming commonplace, as are imitations of the final hole at TPC Sawgrass, and there is a striking resemblance to this template with the last hole on the Olazábal Course, water again threatening throughout on the left.

▶ When Olazábal visited his course during construction in 2002 he was told that his and four other courses had to be finished within one year. They were – some 3,000 workers and 600 machines were brought in to do the work.

ABOVE LEFT *The 16th green on the Faldo Course bears a striking resemblance to the 17th at TPC at Sawgrass.*

BELOW LEFT *Designers have been given almost free rein – this is the imaginative 6th hole on the Ozaki Course.*

CARD OF THE COURSE

Hole	Distance (yards)	Par
1	447	4
2	175	3
3	548	5
4	405	4
5	176	3
6	476	4
7	566	5
8	214	3
9	573	5
Out	3,580	36
10	404	4
11	568	5
12	457	4
13	241	3
14	401	4
15	580	5
16	432	4
17	197	3
18	460	4
In	3,740	36
Total	7,320	72

'This is truly a wonderful course.'

COLIN MONTGOMERIE

SPOILT FOR CHOICE

With 12 courses available, visitors are
spoilt for choice at this astonishing resort.
Notwithstanding the appeal of the
Olazábal Course, many will want to sample
the Nicklaus Course, which hosted the
World Cup in 1995. Possibly the toughest
is the Norman Course, rated one of the
hardest in Asia. The Sorenstam Course,
designed by the first female professional
to play against the men of the PGA Tour,
is quite long enough to keep even them in
check. David Leadbetter has a reputation
as one of the foremost teachers in world
golf. No, his course is not an 'academy
course'. It is every bit as long and
demanding as the rest.

ABOVE *On the 10th, on
the Olazábal Course, it is
better to be on the left
side of the fairway, skirting
these prolific bunkers, to
open up the approach
to the green.*

RIGHT *Sand is present on
the 15th – the signature
hole on the Olazábal
Course – in profusion, too,
but in most cases the
bunkers will save the ball
from finding the water.*

Blue Canyon

Canyon Course, Blue Canyon Country Club, Phuket, Thailand

Thailand is awash with golf courses, some good, some very good. The most celebrated of them all is Blue Canyon, a country club with two brilliant courses, situated in a heavenly spot looking out on to the blue waters of the Andaman Sea, with the Phang Nga mountains creating an inviting terrestrial backdrop. It is fabulously beautiful, but it was not always so. In former times this was a tin mine and rubber plantation.

When it was decided to develop a golf course here, Yoshikazu Kato was engaged as course architect, with a brief to keep the shifting of earth to a minimum and to utilize the natural features of the property. He had been given a helping hand with honouring his brief because huge quantities of earth had already been moved in the tin-mining days and the abandoned workings had filled with the rainwater that falls so abundantly in Thailand to form a network of lakes and ponds. In this climate the rapidly growing vegetation also assists in softening the once stark features. Kato began with the Canyon Course, which was built in 1991. The Lakes Course followed in 1999 and more than lives up to its name – there are water hazards on 17 of the 18 holes.

TIGER TRIUMPHANT

The 1994 Johnnie Walker Classic was played on the Canyon Course. Greg Norman stormed round the course on the final day in 64 for victory. Finishing in a tie for 34th place was a young amateur, Tiger Woods. Woods, now a professional, returned to Blue Canyon for the 1998 Johnnie Walker Classic. He began the last round nine shots behind the leader, Ernie Els, dug deep and caught up with Els on the final green. Woods won the play-off. It was an immensely popular victory, not least because Tiger's mother is herself from Thailand.

The Canyon Course

After a reasonably straightforward opening hole, water is encountered for the first time on the 2nd hole, a par 3 of some length. On the 3rd a huge calabash tree, standing in the middle of the fairway, confronts the golfer. Which way round it do you go? Accuracy off the tee and precise approach shots to tiered greens are called for on the otherwise fairly short par 4s going to the turn, while the stiff par 5s are a foretaste of the challenges ahead.

The sea views from the 10th tee are superb while the hole itself is a manageable dogleg to the left. Then comes a 600-yard/549-m monster of a par 5, with water adding complications for the long hitter. Water is present on the next hole as well, and there are strategic decisions concerning water to be made on the par-3 14th, with its kidney-shaped island green, and the 15th, too. The 17th, squeezed between trees to the left and water to the right, is an outstanding short hole, while the water-troubled 18th ensures that the pressure is kept up right to the very end of this delightful course.

LEFT *The 14th is a deceptive hole, playing shorter than you think because of the big drop from tee to green, and it can be complicated by crosswinds.*

BELOW *The strong finishing hole, with its drive over water and cunningly sloped green.*

'One of the best I have ever played on.'

TIGER WOODS, JOHNNIE
WALKER CLASSIC, 1998

CARD OF THE COURSE

Hole	Distance (yards)	Par
1	390	4
2	218	3
3	449	4
4	407	4
5	398	4
6	556	5
7	205	3
8	412	4
9	561	5
Out	3,596	36
10	392	4
11	600	5
12	440	4
13	390	4
14	194	3
15	586	5
16	357	4
17	221	3
18	403	4
In	3,583	36
Total	7,179	72

New South Wales

New South Wales Golf Club, Matraville, New South Wales, Australia

Australia's largest city, Sydney, is blessed with surprisingly few great courses. The one really exciting course it possesses is to be found high on the cliffs overlooking Botany Bay, at the New South Wales Golf Club. The views are stupendous, the course is rugged and when the wind is up (as it usually is) it can be an absolute brute. But who could begrudge a course its difficulty when the experience is undeniably so uplifting?

Impatient golfers cannot wait to reach the seaside holes, but getting there is no easy matter, with the 2nd a tough par 3 and the 3rd a mystifying hole played blind over a huge sand dune. In an era of golf made easy by the overuse of bulldozers and earth-movers, it is heartening to find such a throwback to the past left intact.

Australia's Pebble Beach?

Although the New South Wales course cannot compete with Pebble Beach for the number of seaside holes it possesses, the quality of them is comparable, starting at the 5th. A magnificent seascape awaits the golfer arriving on this tee, and the player's prowess is immediately called into question. Can you clear the ridge crossing the fairway a driver's length away? If you cannot, you will be faced with a daunting second shot played blind across the ridge with an unknown fate on the far side. Those with the strength to clear the ridge from the tee will enjoy many precious yards of extra roll beyond it, bringing the green in easy reach of two shots. Whatever your golfing ability, and your score on this hole notwithstanding, you would be an unfeeling golfer if you left this green without a spring in your step.

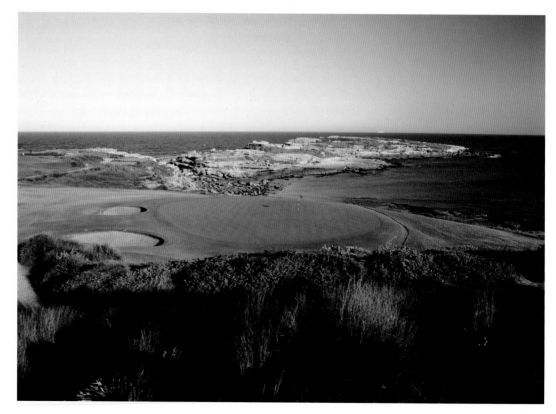

RIGHT *The 6th, viewed from behind the green, is played from a tee on the rocks stretching into Botany Bay, where Captain Cook landed in April 1770.*

▶ The name Alister MacKenzie stands out from the credits list at New South Wales, but MacKenzie was quite restrained in his alterations here, for the original routing was excellent. For that vision, Australian Eric Apperly, an accomplished amateur golfer, must be given due prominence.

RIGHT *For the first-time visitor the 3rd is a perplexing hole, a sharp dogleg on which the right line from the tee is hard to assess.*

CARD OF THE COURSE

Hole	Distance (yards)	Par	Hole	Distance (yards)	Par
1	321	4	10	394	4
2	202	3	11	163	3
3	416	4	12	527	5
4	428	4	13	410	4
5	512	5	14	353	4
6	194	3	15	407	4
7	411	4	16	441	4
8	552	5	17	167	3
9	372	4	18	548	5
Out	3,408	36	In	3,410	36
			Total	6,818	72

The 5th is followed by a short hole surpassing any at Pebble Beach for its dramatic setting, played from a tee low on the rocks over the pounding ocean waves to a green set in a fold of ground on the far side. Golf does not get much better than this!

The most demanding golf, however, is still to come. A stretch of tough par 4s from the 13th to the 16th has the ability to wreck a promising scorecard, so late in the round that there is no chance of rehabilitation. The raised 13th green is extraordinarily hard to attack, while the 14th is one of those rare short par 4s that are rendered little easier by the advent of modern clubs and balls. On the 15th it is the tee shot that puts fear into the heart of many golfers, with an uncompromising drive and no room for error. Any skirmish with the dunes on the 16th is likely to lead to at least one dropped shot.

This stretch may well be the toughest sequence of holes in Australia, particularly so when the wind probes the golfer's technique and resolve, remorselessly revealing the slightest defect. The short 17th is very exposed to the wind, too, while the final hole rewards the stronger hitter.

Royal Melbourne

Royal Melbourne

West Course, Royal Melbourne Golf Club, Black Rock, Victoria, Australia

The Royal Melbourne Golf Club has been – and still is – the most influential golf club in Australian golf. The man who made it so was a visitor, none other than Dr Alister MacKenzie. He had been sent by the R&A following a request from Royal Melbourne seeking advice on the laying out of a new course. MacKenzie arrived in October 1926, staying for two months, during which time he also visited a number of other courses, making suggestions for improvements to these courses, too.

MacKenzie's lasting influence was his recruitment of 1924 Australian Amateur champion and Royal Melbourne member, Alex Russell, and the club's greenkeeper, 'Mick' Morcom. MacKenzie was not going to be in Australia long enough to oversee the changes he suggested for so many clubs, nor would he be around to supervise at Royal Melbourne. Russell and Morcom quickly assimilated MacKenzie's architectural principles and were able to carry out a revolution in strategic design – and bunker design in particular – that has lasted to this day, especially in the Melbourne sand belt.

Model bunkers

Some years ago, when Nick Faldo, then just starting out in the golf design business, was in Australia to play in a number of tournaments, he was not to be found on the practice range in his down time. He was seen, instead, standing in, walking around, photographing and measuring many of the bunkers at Royal Melbourne, so impressed was he by their enormous variety and the huge influence they still exert on playing strategy, even though modern professionals are so expert at bunker play.

RIGHT *Both courses intertwine engagingly at Royal Melbourne. Viewed from the back of the 2nd green on the East Course, the famous 6th on the West can be seen stretching into the distance on the right.*

The bunkers are only part of the story, for the real genius of the West Course is the way MacKenzie routed the course to take maximum advantage of the topography of the site. Take, for instance, the sequence of holes from the 3rd to the 10th, which makes brilliant use of two big sandhills and two smaller ones. The 4th is a magnificent hole, whether played as a short par 5 or ultra-long par 4, with a drive over cavernous bunkers to a distant hilltop, followed by a long second shot, very likely played from a hanging lie, along a curving fairway to a heavily bunkered, distant green. Then comes the 5th, as gorgeous a short hole as you could wish to find, and the 6th is one of the world's great two-shot holes, with a drive over serious bunkers to set up an approach shot to a deliciously bunkered, ledge green cradled in the dunes of one of the bigger hills.

Little attention is usually given to the short 7th, which is a better hole for being routed up a hill rather than over an adjacent pond, while the 8th green is unreceptive, being sloped down towards the back and attendant bunkers. A mid-length par 4 follows, with a tricky pitch uphill to the green, and then comes the fabulous 10th, as wonderful a short par 4 as you could hope to find, tempting the long hitter to drive the green and punishing even the slightest failure mercilessly. It remains a great hole despite our superior clubs and balls.

▶ For tournaments, a composite course is drawn from the West and East Courses, keeping play within the boundaries of the main club grounds and avoiding road crossings.

▶ Royal Melbourne's founders included a number of Scots: John Bruce, Tom Finlay and Hugh Playfair, from St Andrews, and William Knox and Tom Brentnall from Musselburgh.

CARD OF THE COURSE

Hole	Distance (yards)	Par
1	429	4
2	480	5
3	354	4
4	470	5
5	176	3
6	428	4
7	148	3
8	379	4
9	416	4
Out	3,280	36
10	305	4
11	455	4
12	476	5
13	147	3
14	366	4
15	467	5
16	221	3
17	439	4
18	433	4
In	3,309	36
Total	6,589	72

'This is one of the great courses in the world, but there is a fear factor to it.'

NICK FALDO

Cape Kidnappers

Cape Kidnappers

Cape Kidnappers Golf Course, Hawke's Bay, North Island, New Zealand

For many years New Zealand has been something of a golfing sleeper. Given the natural advantages of climate and setting few courses realized their true potential, Paraparaumu Beach being one of the exceptions. Now there are two spectacular modern courses – Kauri Cliffs and Cape Kidnappers – that have raised the bar enormously, just as their American developer, Julian Robertson, has raised the bar in golf tourism in New Zealand.

The name, Cape Kidnappers, is sufficient to suggest that here are to be found stunning seascapes and any number of fabulous holes exploiting them. But the key to maximizing the potential of a site of this kind is what you do with the rest of the course. It would be disappointing to have to play dull holes on dull ground simply as a means of getting to the exceptional holes. By choosing Tom Doak as the designer, Robertson was on to a winner, for Doak is a master at routing

a golf course, ensuring that every hole is of golfing interest, that there is a good balance between sorts and styles of holes and that the entire course is memorable. He and his team walked the site many times before setting to work, taking in the enormity of the task, getting to know every inch of the ground and simply coming to terms with the magnificent canvas he had been given. Doak was able to exploit his talent for locating stunning green sites.

RIGHT *On the edge of the earth, the 12th green is just one of a number of stunningly sited targets presented to the golfer during the round.*

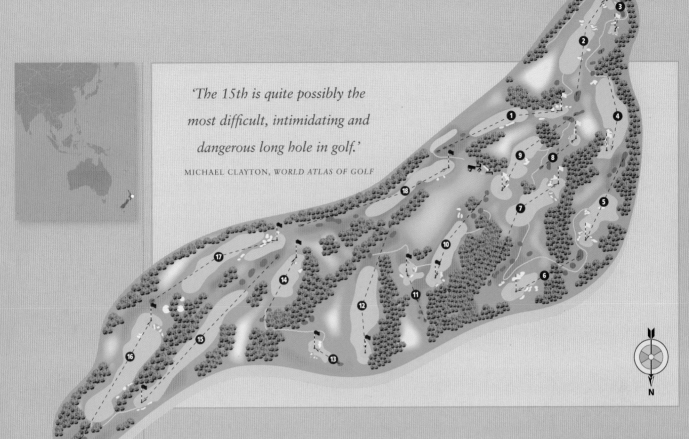

'The 15th is quite possibly the most difficult, intimidating and dangerous long hole in golf.'

MICHAEL CLAYTON, *WORLD ATLAS OF GOLF*

Width and options

Doak has rebelled against the 'total' architecture of many of his contemporaries: not for him narrow fairways that call for target golf on every shot. Instead, where possible, Doak gives you width, just as Alister MacKenzie did in the early 20th century. And, just as MacKenzie's greens were defended cleverly so that you had to conjure up a different kind of approach shot depending on where exactly you were on the fairway, Doak requires you to use your imagination by giving you choice.

You are, for instance, given a lovely wide fairway on the 1st, tempting you into a big drive. But the green is angled across the line of the fairway and cleverly bunkered. Unless you are in the correct part of the fairway you may find you have no shot to the green. You have to do your homework – on every hole: you cannot blast your way round here.

Cape Kidnappers would be a fine course even if it consisted solely of holes comparable with the early ones, but it is at the 12th that it becomes exceptional, with a string of breathtaking clifftop holes. And that 12th green – sitting on the skyline twixt heaven and hell! It is followed by a short hole on the very edge of the cliffs and a clever drive-and-pitch hole made particularly devilish by a demon of a pot-bunker. This gives way to a 650-yard/594-m par 5 of incredible beauty and great treachery: to the left a vertiginous drop to the ocean; to the right a ball-swallowing ravine. Although a stroke might be rescued at the 16th, the two closing holes are decidedly tough, with Doak making you think until the very last putt has dropped.

▶ In 2007 *Golf Digest* magazine rated Cape Kidnappers the 10th best course in the world outside the United States – some accolade for a course opened as recently as 2004!

▶ The name Cape Kidnappers was given to this spot in 1769 by Captain Cook following a Maori's attempt to abduct his cabin boy from his ship, HMS *Endeavour*.

CARD OF THE COURSE

Hole	Distance (yards)	Par
1	440	4
2	540	5
3	215	3
4	544	5
5	420	4
6	225	3
7	453	4
8	182	3
9	403	4
Out	3,422	35
10	430	4
11	224	3
12	460	4
13	130	3
14	348	4
15	650	5
16	500	5
17	463	4
18	480	4
In	3,685	36
Total	7,107	71

ROBERTSON'S VISION

Julian Robertson's other contribution to
state-of-the-art golf in New Zealand is
Kauri Cliffs on the North Island. As at Cape
Kidnappers there are stunning seascapes
from this clifftop course, which was laid out
by David Harman, the Florida-based golf
course designer. No fewer than 15 holes
look out to sea, although some of the best
holes are inland, such as the par-5 4th. The
first skirmish with the ocean comes at the
par-3 7th, an all-or-nothing carry over an
abyss. There is an invigorating sequence
of clifftop holes on the back nine, too,
from the 14th to the 17th. Obviously, there
are similarities between the two courses,
because of their spectacular locations,
but what makes a fascinating comparison
is in the fine detail work of the two very
different architects.

RIGHT *The spectacular setting
of the stretch of holes from the
14th to the 17th is wonderfully
captured in this aerial photograph.
The 14th and 17th greens are in
the foreground.*

▶▶▶ Index

Acknowledgements

The publishers would like to thank the following for permission to reproduce copyright material:

Celtic Manor Resort, p 44

Corbis/Tony Roberts, p 89.

Getty Images, p 62; /David Alexander, pp 10, 11; /Stan Badz/PGA, p 74; /David Cannon, pp 2, 6, 6–7, 7, 16, 20, 22, 23, 26, 28, 38, 40, 42–43, 46, 47, 50, 76, 78, 80, 81, 100, 114, 126, 136, 137, 138, 140, 142–43; /Chris Condon/PGA, p 72; /Richard Heathcoate, pp 127, 132, 132–33; /Harry How, pp 58, 62–63, 63, 68; /Image Source Black, p 4–5; /Ross Kinnaird, p 74–75; /Warren Little, pp 96, 97; /Steve Munday, pp 9, 32; /Paul Severn, p 112–13.

Hotel Transamérica Ilha de Comandatuba, pp 92, 93.

Karen Country Club, pp 120, 121.

Kiawah Island Golf Resort, pp 64, 65.

Iain Lowe Photography, p 24–25.

Brian Morgan, pp 56, 85, 88, 128, 129.

Ran Morrissett/GolfClubAtlas.com, pp 83, 90.

Mark Rowlinson, p 108.

Phil Sheldon Golf Picture Library, pp 8, 30, 31, 34, 52–53, 59, 60, 70, 71, 113, 117, 118, 122; /Bob Atkins, p 48; /Richard Castka, pp 130 above, 130 below, 135; /Karina Hoskyns, pp 104–105, 105.

Stefan von Stengel pp 82, 84, 86–87, 94, 95, 98, 99, 102, 106, 107, 110, 116, 124, 124–25, 134.